Jim Blankenship, CFP®, EA

A 401(k) Owner's Manual

Your Guide To
the 401(k) Employer Retirement Plan

Copyright © 2020, 2022 by Jim Blankenship, CFP®

A 401(k) Owner's Manual

By Jim Blankenship, CFP®

ISBN 978-1671251038 / 1671251038

All rights reserved solely by the author. The author guarantees all contents are original and do not infringe upon the legal rights of any other person or work. No part of this book may be reproduced in any form without the permission of the author. The views expressed in this book are solely the views of the author and do not represent the views of the publisher.

Reproduction or translation of any part of this work beyond that permitted in Section 107 or 108 of the 1976 United States Copyright Act without the permission of the copyright owner is unlawful.

Use of the words "IRS", "Internal Revenue Service", "the Service", "DOL", "Department of Labor", or "United States Department of the Treasury" in this work should not be in any way interpreted or construed as approval, endorsement or authorization by the Internal Revenue Service, the United States Department of Labor, the United States Department of the Treasury, or any other unit of government, or that the author has some connection with or authorization from the Internal Revenue Service, the United States Department of Labor, the United States Department of the Treasury, or any other unit of government. It must be understood that all specific facts and rules explained in this book are freely available from the Internal Revenue Service and the Department of Labor.

Every effort has been made to ensure this publication is as accurate and complete as possible. However, no representations or warranties are made with respect to the accuracy or completeness of the contents of this book. It is not the intent of this publication or its author to provide professional tax, investment or legal advice. The strategies contained herein may not be suitable for your situation. You should consult with a professional where appropriate. This publication should only be used as a general guideline and not as the ultimate source of information regarding retirement plans.

Requests for permission or further information should be directed to the author via email at Jim@BlankenshipFinancial.com.

Cover design by Jessea Negless of StreetFire Designs –
www.streetfiredesigns.com

About the author

Jim Blankenship is a financial planner based in New Berlin, Illinois. Through his Fee-Only financial planning practice, Jim provides unbiased financial advice to individuals from all walks of life.

Jim Blankenship, CFP®, EA

Jim@BlankenshipFinancial.com

About the series

The Owner's Manual series has always been about helping others to understand some of the most common but terribly complicated facets of our financial lives. Hopefully I've accomplished this goal, at least to a point.

From what I hear from readers, I think I'm on the right track. It's gratifying to learn that I have somehow had an impact on the lives of so many people over the years. We all want to somehow leave behind a legacy from our life's work.

> *The great use of life is to spend it for something that will outlast it.*
> *—William James*

Here are the other books in the Owner's Manual series:

An IRA Owner's Manual
A Social Security Owner's Manual
A Medicare Owner's Manual

Also by Jim Blankenship:
Social Security for the Suddenly Single

Dedication

I dedicate this book and all of my writings to my lovely wife Nancy. You make it all worthwhile.

Acknowledgements

I'm always amazed by my friends' and colleagues' lending their time and talents so selflessly to help out with my projects. I know that time is a valuable commodity for everyone these days, and yet these folks have given time and again to help me out. I can't possibly show you how grateful I am to all of you.

Specifically, the following people have spent time reviewing and lending comments to help make my incomprehensive drivel into something worth reading:

David McPherson
Dave Barnett
Steve Highsmith
Tracy St John
Skip Fleming
Lee Slater

In addition to those folks, I need to acknowledge the members of the Garrett Planning Network and in particular their leader Sheryl Garrett, for unwittingly standing in as the giants upon whose shoulders I attempt to stand. The FinCon community has provided many thousands of lines of fine examples to guide me along the way.

Many thanks as well to my friend Roger Wohlner, who lent his talents to the foreword for this book. Roger, you've always been not only a stellar example to emulate, but also good friend and confidante through the years.

Lastly, a special shout out to my business partner Sterling Raskie, for always being willing to listen to my crazy ramblings and apply a voice of reason when needed. Your broad knowledge is indispensable, and you always have an appropriate movie quote mashup to apply to the situation. If that doesn't clear things up I know you'll put a soundtrack on it (probably from Rush) and all will suddenly be aligned.

Table of contents

Foreword xv
Introduction xix
Part 1: History of 401(k) plans 1
  1. History of the 401(k) plan 1
  2. Evolution of 401(k) plans 7
Part 2: Fundamentals of 401(k) plans 11
  3. What is a 401(k) plan? 11
  4. Features of 401(k) Plans 15
  5. The Best 401(k) Plan 27
  6. Defined Contribution vs Defined Benefit 33
  7. Withdrawals from your 401(k) plan 35
  8. Nondiscrimination Rules 39
Part 3: Benefits of 401(k) plan participation 45
  9. Automated Savings 45
  10. Employer Match 51
  11. Vesting of Employer Match 55
  12. Dollar-Cost Averaging 59
  13. 401(k) loans 63
Part 4: Roth 401(k) plan 69
  14. Roth 401(k) plan Basics 69
  15. Contributions to Roth 401(k) plan 77
  16. Company matching in a Roth 401(k) plan 81
  17. Distributions from Roth 401(k) plan 83
Part 5: Distributions from a 401(k) plan 85
  18. Distributions at or after retirement age 85
  19. Required Minimum Distributions (RMD) 91
  20. Distributions before retirement age 99
  21. Rollovers 103
  22. Taxes on your 401(k) plan withdrawal 109
  23. Early Distribution Penalty Exceptions 113
  24. Net Unrealized Appreciation (NUA) 123
  25. 72(t) SOSEPP Distributions 129
  26. 401(k) loan versus withdrawal 137
Part 6: Other employer retirement plans 141
  27. 403(b) Plans 141
  28. 457(b) (governmental) Plans 145
  29. Solo 401(k) 149
  30. Inherited 401(k) Plan 153

31. Other Retirement Plans 161
Part 7: Conclusion 167
    32. Did the Advent of 401(k) Plans Hurt Americans? 167
    33. Future of the 401(k) plan..169
    34. Integrating the 401(k) Into Your Financial Plan 173

Foreword

It's hard to read a financial publication or watch a cable financial news show these days without some discussion of the challenges facing current and future retirees. Whether it's the projected shortfalls in Social Security, depending upon who you believe, high medical costs or just the fact that we are all living longer, retirement for today's Boomers and generations to follow is more challenging than for our parents and grandparents.

Add to this the fact that the pensions that were common for retirees in prior generations are rapidly becoming a thing of the past, and we all realize that our retirement is on us. In large measure the quality and the financial stability of our retirement years will be dependent on the amount we save for retirement.

The main retirement savings vehicles for most of us are employer-sponsored retirement plans like the 401(k).

On the one hand, plans like 401(k)s, 403(b)s, 457 plans and others seem simple. You put in part of your salary each pay period and choose one or more investments from the investment menu offered. At retirement you take your money out, pay taxes on the withdrawals (unless the account is a Roth) and live happily ever after.

Unfortunately, 401(k) plans are anything but simple for those who use them to invest their savings for retirement. In fact, these and similar plans are not only complicated and confusing for those participating in them, many financial advisors express similar levels of confusion when dealing with the plans their clients have at work in the course of providing advice to them.

A 401(k) Owner's Manual provides a comprehensive user's guide for anyone involved with a 401(k), 403(b), 457 plan, solo 401(k)s and for those inheriting a 401(k).

Jim takes the 401(k) from its inception in the late 1970s through today and into the future. As someone who has been involved with 401(k) plans as an advisor to several plans, as an advisor to individuals who have had them in their jobs, as someone trying to manage my wife's and my own accounts and as a financial writer covering this topic, this book is a must own for me.

As is the case with anything Jim does, he covers every aspect of these plans in detail. Readers who want to take a deep dive into the history, workings and uses of 401(k)s can read it cover-to-cover. For others, this is a great reference guide for questions on specific aspects of owning a 401(k) account.

The book covers the whole gamut of issues from how to contribute, to the ins and outs of the employer matches including the all-important issue of vesting. It covers the potential benefits of a Roth account, as well as the critical issues that you need to know when it comes time to withdraw your funds in retirement.

Beyond this, he covers issues that impact plan advisors and sponsors such as the discrimination testing that plans are subject to and special situations like a QDRO stemming from a divorce.

In his introduction, Jim makes the point that "it's on you" referring to our responsibility for our own retirement. This book arms you with your own guide to managing this all-important aspect of your retirement savings. Even if you aren't a finance nerd like me, I think you will find this book to be a must own.

Roger Wohlner, MBA
Financial writer
Financial advisor
RLW Associates, LLC
The Chicago Financial Planner blog
www.TheChicagoFinancialPlanner.com

Introduction

It must be understood at the outset that as the author of this book I have no connection with or authorization from the Internal Revenue Service, the United States Department of Labor, or the United States Department of the Treasury. Use of the words "IRS", "Internal Revenue Service", "the Service", "DOL", "Department of Labor", or "United States Department of the Treasury" in this work should not be in any way interpreted or construed as approval, endorsement or authorization by the Internal Revenue Service, the United States Department of Labor, the United States Department of the Treasury, or any other unit of government, or that the author has some connection with or authorization from the Internal Revenue Service, the United States Department of Labor, the United States Department of the Treasury, or any other unit of government.

The facts in this publication are freely available from the Internal Revenue Service or the United States Department of Labor. The organization, interpretation, and explanation of these facts has been developed over years of study of the facts and rules of the system. It is the organization, interpretation and explanations that provide the value in this work.

We all know that we should save money for a rainy day, a message we've received since we were little ones. A 401(k) can be a very important and useful component of your savings process. It's more important nowadays than ever before.

It's on you

Back in the olden days when the earth was still cooling, employees could count on (or at least were told they could count on) a pension benefit from their employer upon retirement. This pension plan provided a safety net that allowed the employee to go into retirement with relatively little concern about whether there would be enough money to live on.

However, the pension plan has gone the way of the buggy whip for most employees these days. Relatively few employers (with the exception of many governmental entities) offer a traditional defined benefit pension plan any more, and many times, if a pension is offered at all, the amount of the pension available has been cut back drastically. This means that it's up to you to provide for your retirement income – and one way to do this is to save money in a 401(k) plan. Saving money into a 401(k) plan can provide you with a tax-advantaged way to set yourself up for the future as well as to ease your mind going into retirement.

A good habit

Saving in any form is generally a good habit. Saving using a 401(k) plan is a low-impact way to do this, because your money is deducted from your paycheck before you get your hands on it, automatically, every payday. Once you've set up your contributions, you don't have to remember to make a savings contribution, it's done automatically for you.

Plus, since it's not easy to take money out of your 401(k) plan (it's generally disallowed while still employed) and can be quite costly if you do take money out before retirement, you're much more likely to leave the money alone until you need it in retirement. This helps to generate self-discipline with regard to savings. It's a good habit to get into, thinking of your savings as untouchable during your accumulation years.

Best avenue to success

It might be argued that choosing the best, most successful, fastest growing investment is the best way to grow your retirement account to the greatest amount. Time and time again however, it has been proven that the greatest determinant of your retirement savings success is the amount that you set aside. First and foremost, the more you have set aside, the more that fast-growing investment has to build upon.

Another very important determinant of success in retirement saving is to start early, and maintain the savings habit over time. This is because time, when used to compound savings, is very powerful. If your investments return 6% on average per year, after the first year a $1,000 contribution is worth $1,060. After the second year at the same rate, when you contribute another $1,000 to the account and last year's money compounds as well, you would have a total of $2,183.60 – from a total investment of $2,000. After 10 years of this routine, you've deferred $10,000, but your account has grown to $13,971.64.

The 401(k) plan is an excellent vehicle to use to take advantage of saving significant amounts of money and allowing time, compounding interest, and returns to work hard for your retirement.

Throughout this book I refer to 401(k) plans specifically, and in some cases the rules discussed may apply to other types of employer-provided retirement plans – specifically 403(b) and 457(b) plans. This is because Section 401(k) of the Internal Revenue Code has been used as the model for these other, similar plans. In Part 6 we'll briefly review the distinctions for these other plans. Refer to those chapters for a starting point if you need information about your specific plan. This book is not intended to be an exhaustive resource for those plans, so you should include other sources in your study of those plans.

Part 1: History of 401(k) plans

1. History of the 401(k) plan

Back in 1978, the year of 3 Popes, Congress passed the Revenue Act of 1978, which included a provision that became Internal Revenue Code section 401(k).

However, the 401(k) has roots going back several decades earlier, with many different rulings (Hicks v. US, Revenue Ruling 56-497 and Revenue Ruling 63-180 being among the most prominent), providing the groundwork for the specialized tax treatment of salary deferrals that Section 401(k) enabled.

More groundwork for the 401(k) as we know it was laid with the passage of the Employee Retirement Income Security Act (ERISA) of 1974. With ERISA, the Treasury Department was restricted from putting forth a particular set of regulations that would have reduced or eliminated the tax-deferral benefits of certain deferred compensation plans. After the Treasury Department withdrew the proposed regulations in 1978, the way was cleared to introduce the 401(k) plan (as we know it) with the Revenue Act.

This particular section of the Code enabled profit-sharing plans to adopt cash or deferred arrangements, or CODAs, funded via pre-tax salary deferral contributions. When the 401(k) code section became effective in January 1980, and the IRS proposed regulations for Section 401(k) in late 1981, the idea came forth to replace existing bonus arrangements with the new tax-deferred alternative. The real kicker that caused the 401(k) plan to garner interest by employers was the ability to save on taxes while still maintaining competitiveness with the earlier bonus plans - and the employer matching arrangement of 401(k) plans did just that.

Several large corporations very quickly began replacing after-tax thrift plans with the new 401(k) plan and adding 401(k) options to existing profit-sharing and stock bonus plans. The new 401(k)-type of plan provided the employee with deferred taxation on income diverted into the plans, while providing the employers with the ability to make significant matching contributions, also on a tax-favored basis.

The Tax Reform Act of 1984 enacted rules for nondiscrimination testing in the 401(k) plans. This means that highly-compensated employees can't receive benefit from the plans if non-highly-compensated employees aren't participating in the plans to an acceptable degree.

Then the 1986 Tax Reform Act further tightened the nondiscrimination restrictions and set the maximum annual allowable amount of deferral of compensation by employees at $7,000. Up to this point, there was only an annual limit on all contributions by both the employer and employee, which was set at $30,000 from 1987 through 2003. These amounts have gradually increased to 2022's levels of $20,500 for regular deferral by employees (plus a catch-up contribution of $6,500 for employees over age 50) and a total annual limit for all contributions of $67,500 ($61,000 plus $6,500 catch up contributions).

A 20% mandatory withholding requirement for distributions from 401(k) plans was added with the 1992 Unemployment Compensation Amendments. This requirement applies to distributions that are not rolled over into another retirement plan, including an IRA.

In 1996, the passage of the Small Business Job Protection Act provided an additional boost to participation in 401(k) plans with the elimination of limits on contributions that could be made to a retirement plan by an employee who is also participating in a regular defined benefit pension plan.

One more piece of legislation that had a huge impact on 401(k) plans was the Economic Growth and Tax Relief Reconciliation Act of 2001 (EGTRRA). This act bumped up the total annual maximum contribution by employers and employees (it had been frozen at $30,000 since 1987), as well as adding the "catch-up" contribution provision. The catch-up contribution provision allows participants who are age 50 or older an additional amount to defer into 401(k) plans annually, not limited by the annual maximum contribution amount. The catch-up contribution was set at $3,000 initially and has been indexed to the 2022 limit of $6,500.

EGTRRA also introduced the Roth 401(k) feature, which allows participants to elect a designated separate account within the 401(k) plan that accepts salary deferrals on an after-tax basis. The account then provides for tax-free treatment (like a Roth IRA) for qualified distributions.

After EGTRRA, the Pension Protection Act of 2006 came along, which made permanent certain provisions of EGTRRA (originally some provisions were set to expire in 2010), as well as providing methods for employers to automatically enroll employees in 401(k) plans and choose default investments. The purpose of these provisions was to bolster participation in 401(k) plans and facilitate the best use of these plans.

The 2013 American Taxpayer Relief Act (ATRA) provided a method for converting "regular" 401(k) account funds to Roth 401(k) accounts. Previously, a participant in a 401(k) plan could only convert funds from the regular account to the Roth account if he or she was in a position to otherwise distribute funds from the account. Generally, this means that the employee/participant has left the job associated with the 401(k) or has reached a retirement age set by the plan administrator. With the new rules provided by ATRA, these conversions could be undertaken by a currently-employed participant of any age. Not all plans offer this feature.

Most recently, the Setting Every Community Up for Retirement Enhancement (SECURE) Act introduced several new features. Among these new features are a later beginning date for Requirement Minimum Distributions (72 instead of 70½), reduction of the distribution period for most non-spouse beneficiaries to 10 years (instead of lifetime), the ability of long-term part-time employees to participate in a 401(k) plan, an exception to early distributions from 401(k) plans for birth or adoptions, and provisions to encourage employees toward use of annuity products for lifetime distributions, among other provisions.

2. Evolution of 401(k) plans

The 401(k) plan began as somewhat of an accident. The Internal Revenue Code section was included to address uncertainty about the tax status of profit-sharing plans for large corporations. These profit-sharing plans had been in existence for several decades. During that time, income within these plans was deferred, but had never specifically been addressed in the Internal Revenue Code. During the 1970's, Congress considered eliminating this favorable treatment but then reversed course – and ensuing legislation in 1978 brought about section 401(k) to the Code. This section was designed to limit access to the deferred profit-sharing account by those few executives who took advantage of the plans.

It was anticipated that code section 401(k) would only apply to that small handful of companies that had these profit-sharing plans in existence. But what happened next was completely unforeseen.

A benefits consultant named Ted Benna, working for the Johnson Companies, undertook a new interpretation of the code section such that it would apply to all full-time employees. In the past, profit-sharing deferral plans were limited in scope to only the highest-paid executives. The new code had no specific limit on participants. With a few minor tweaks to the proposed rules, which Benna recommended to the IRS and which were accepted and applied, this type of account could be made widely available for nearly all employees.

Benna's plan was the first to provide a method for all full-time employees to readily defer a portion of regular salary (as well as bonuses and other compensation) into a tax-deferred account. Deferring income into these accounts allowed for reduction of the employee's taxable income (but only ordinary income tax; Social Security and Medicare taxes still apply).

After a few short years, legislation was added to provide for payroll deduction (beginning in 1981), which made participating in the plans even easier for employees.

Later, in 1984, rules were added that provided for nondiscrimination testing. These rules limit the amount of salary the highest paid employees in a company can defer, based upon participation by employees from all categories and compensation levels. These rules were designed to keep high-paid executives from taking advantage of the plans at the cost of lower paid employees. In response to these rules, companies began offering more generous matching contributions to incent employees to participate. This also promoted sharing the profits of the corporation with the entire employee base.

These days, 401(k) plans have evolved to a point where companies have the option to automatically enroll employees in the plans, which further increases participation. This encourages savings by employees at all levels and provides for a better chance that the plan will pass the nondiscrimination rules for its executive employees. The auto-enrollment option typically utilizes a target-date investment matching the employee's expected retirement date as the default investment.

Employees can opt out of the auto-enrollment plans, but they must explicitly do so. They can also change the investment elections and increase or decrease the amount of the contribution as they see fit. Of course, this must be within the bounds of the plan's inherent rules. Each plan has much flexibility in adopting various features and benefits for participants.

In addition to the auto-enrollment feature, many plans nowadays also provide an auto-increase option. This option allows an employee to begin contributions at the rate of (for example) 1% of salary. After a year, with the auto-increase feature, the contribution rate is automatically increased to 2%. This increase continues each year by a set rate, until the maximum deferral amount is reached or the employee opts out of the auto-increase. This feature helps employees reach savings goals by automatically and gradually increasing the amount of contribution each year. In addition, with the incremental nature of the increases, the impact of reduced take-home pay is spread out over time.

Another item that has evolved over time is the list of investment options available to participants. Originally 401(k) plans had only two investment options: a stock fund (typically the employer's stock) and a fund that could be likened to a money market, usually a guaranteed investment contract of some sort. Soon participants complained that this was too restrictive, and so over time the number of choices has increased, in some cases dramatically.

The problem with more choices is that participants in the plans can become confused — analysis paralysis, it has been referred to — and often have difficulty making proper decisions about how to invest in the plans. Due to this complexity many folks simply decline to participate at all. Others opt for investing choices that do not meet their investment risk profile properly — such as investing all deferrals in company stock or a money market, for example.

Today, many plans have opted to provide significant numbers of investment choices, which is good, but the participants have demonstrated a need for advice. This is being addressed in the form of educational offerings and one-on-one meetings for participants at many companies. Participation in these advice offerings has been tepid but is increasing.

Additionally, many plans have default investment options available, which helps to make the investing process less complicated. Many plans' default investment is a balanced investment choice or a target-date fund of funds. While not necessarily ideal for all investors, this type of investment typically provides good diversification among assets and asset classes with little to no effort by the investor. Target-date funds help with making the adjustment of asset allocation over time as well.

Part 2: Fundamentals of 401(k) plans

3. What is a 401(k) plan?

A 401(k) plan is a special retirement savings account that is provided by your employer. When you choose to participate in a 401(k) plan, you determine an amount of your regular income that you'd like to defer. The deferral can be either a percentage of your income or a specific dollar amount per pay period.

Deferring income means that your take-home pay will be reduced, and a portion of your pay will be set aside (deferred) in the 401(k) account. Once the money has been placed in the 401(k) account, it is invested. Your plan may have many choices for investments, including stock in the company, mutual funds, ETFs (Exchange Traded Funds), and money market funds.

Over time, as your contributions continue to be deferred into the account, and your chosen investments (hopefully) increase in value, your retirement savings balance increases. When you retire, you can withdraw the money from the account (with some restrictions) and you will pay ordinary income tax on the withdrawals.

Many companies offer a matching contribution as well. This means that as you defer money into the

401(k), the company will also place money in the account. This matching is effectively increasing your overall income, even though you have not worked more or gained a raise from the company. Often this is referred to as "free money" – because all you have to do to get this match from your employer is to participate in the 401(k) plan. Some types of plans feature company contributions regardless of the employee participation level.

For example, if you have an annual income of $40,000, and you defer 5% into your 401(k) plan, your take-home pay will be reduced (but not by 5%, more on this later). If the company matches your contributions dollar-for-dollar, they would also place 5% of your income in the 401(k) account.

Your overall income, originally $40,000, is now increased to $42,000 with the employer match. You would not see this increase in your take-home pay (it will actually go down). But your total income, which includes your taxable income ($38,000, which is all you have to pay tax on this year), plus your 401(k) deferral of $2,000 (5%), plus the employer match of $2,000 (5%), which adds up to $42,000.

At the end of the year, you have taxable income of $38,000 plus tax-deferred income of $4,000 in your 401(k) plan.

This is just the basic overview of 401(k) plans and how they work. Next we'll cover the various features that 401(k) plans may have. 401(k) plan administrators have a lot of flexibility and can choose to offer certain features in the plan or not.

4. Features of 401(k) Plans

401(k) plans have many features that vary from plan to plan. Listed here is an overview of many of the common features that 401(k) plans may include. These are not required features; each plan has the choice to provide the option or not. Each company and plan administrator can also place certain restrictions on the features.

Loans

Many 401(k) plans offer a loan feature. This feature provides a method for the plan participant to borrow a limited amount of the funds in the plan, for a limited period of time. By law, these loans can be no more than the lesser of:

- 50% of your total account balance; or
- $50,000

An exception to this limitation is allowed if your plan account balance is less than $20,000. If this is the case, you may be allowed to borrow up to the lesser of:

- $10,000; or
- your total account balance

All loans are subject to approval by the plan administrator.

These loans must be paid back within a period of no more than 5 years from the time of the loan origination. You will be charged interest (by your 401(k) account) for the loan, just the same as with a bank or credit card company. This interest rate is determined by the plan administrator and is generally lower than a comparable unsecured personal loan.

It is also permissible to have more than one loan outstanding at a time, but the total of all loans is limited to the amounts mentioned previously.

Loans are not subject to tax, provided they are paid back in a timely manner. If the loan is not paid back when the employee leaves employment at the company, the loan may become immediately due. If the employee does not pay back the loan within a specified period of time (see Chapter 13 for more details), the outstanding balance is considered a distribution. Taxes will apply to the distribution, and possibly penalties as well.

Hardship withdrawals

Most plans also provide an option for plan participants to make withdrawals from the plan while still employed. One circumstance where an in-service withdrawal is often allowed is in the case of financial hardship experienced by the employee. The plan administrator may require statements of financial worth and other details in order to prove the hardship exists, but this can be a real godsend for folks facing significant financial trials.

Hardship withdrawals are completed distributions (not loans) from the 401(k) plan. As such, these distributions are subject to taxation, and could be subjected to penalties as well, unless an exception applies. See the list of exceptions to this penalty in Chapter 23.

Contribution methods

There are a couple of different ways that you can put money into a 401(k) plan: contributions (deductible or non-deductible) and rollover contributions.

Deductible Contributions refer to the regular deposits of money into your 401(k) account, most often by payroll deduction. The contributions are limited to the lesser of 100% of your income or $20,500 (2022 figure). The contribution amount is adjusted annually.

In addition, your employer may make matching contributions to your 401(k) account. These are typically expressed as a percentage of your income and are based upon your participation in the plan. For example, your employer may make 50% matching contributions on the first 6% of your income that you defer to the account each year.

On top of the regular contribution limit mentioned above, folks who are over age 50 may also make catch-up contributions to their 401(k) accounts. The limit for catch-up contributions for 2022 is $6,500 per year.

Regular contributions to your 401(k) plan are deferred from ordinary income taxation. This is done by salary deferral. The contributed amount reduces the amount of your income that you will pay ordinary income taxes on (and that taxes are withheld for). The tax-deferral only applies to ordinary income tax – your contributions are still subject to Social Security and Medicare tax.

Growth of your funds from investment returns is not taxed each year while in the plan. However, when you withdraw money from the account the regular contributions, employer matching contributions, and growth on those contributions are taxed at ordinary income tax rates.

Non-deductible (after-tax) contributions. In addition to the tax-deferred method of 401(k) contributions, some plans allow for non-deductible contributions in excess of the annual deferral limit. These contributions are treated tax-wise the same as Roth 401(k) contributions (see Chapter 15), but the growth on these contributions is subject to ordinary income tax upon distribution.

You might want to make non-deductible contributions to your 401(k) plan if you have maxed out on all other retirement plan contributions (Roth IRA or traditional IRA, and tax-deferred 401(k) or Roth 401(k)), and you still have money that you'd like to get locked up in your retirement savings.

If you make non-deductible contributions, you'll need to keep good records on your account, especially as you take distributions. You want to ensure that you're not paying tax again on distributions that should be coming to you tax-free.

There's also a dilemma that you must face if you're considering making non-deductible or after-tax contributions to your 401(k). An alternative savings vehicle would be a regular, non-deferred, investment account.

With the non-deferred investment account, your contributions would be similar to the non-deductible 401(k) contributions in that they've already been taxed. The difference is that, with the non-deferred account, your growth in the account is taxed at either dividend or capital gains rates, rather than ordinary income tax rates. Generally, the dividend and capital gains rates will be preferable, that is, lower than ordinary income tax rates. Dividends are taxed in the year that they are earned, while capital gains are taxed when realized, which is when you sell the investment that has inherent capital gains.

But there's yet another feature to your after-tax deferrals to 401(k) that might be the deciding factor: Your after-tax contributions to 401(k) are eligible for direct rollover to a Roth IRA after you've left employment. This action is referred to as a rollover rather than a conversion because it's a direct transfer from the 401(k) to your Roth IRA *with no tax paid on the transfer!*

This is a significant departure from a conversion from either a 401(k) or IRA to a Roth IRA. Those conversions cause you to recognize the converted money as income for ordinary income tax purposes in the year of the conversion/distribution.

Only the actual non-deducted (after-tax) contributions can be rolled over tax-free to a Roth IRA. Any growth on those contributions will be treated the same as the rest of your 401(k) account. But given the fact that the maximum overall contribution amount for a 401(k) is $67,500 in 2022 (versus $27,000 in deductible deferrals), this represents an additional $40,500 contributions that you can make each year, which can later be rolled into your Roth IRA.

In addition, since the Roth IRA itself only allows a $6,000 annual contribution ($7,000 if over age 50, 2022 figures), this strategy gives you a chance to supercharge your Roth IRA balance.

The potential for a huge Roth IRA balance to fuel future tax-free withdrawals is a very attractive option for some folks to consider. This is especially beneficial for someone who otherwise is not allowed (by income level) to contribute money to a Roth IRA.

Rollover contributions come from previously deferred funds. As an example, you may have just left a job where you had a 401(k) plan, and you wish to combine that account with your new employer's 401(k) plan. IF your new plan administrator allows rollovers into the plan, you can request that the old plan's administrator transfer your balance from the old plan to the new 401(k) plan. Not all plans allow rollovers.

In another example, you might have an IRA that you'd like to move into your existing 401(k) plan. Again, IF your current plan administrator allows rollovers, you may be eligible to transfer the IRA into your 401(k) plan.

There are limits to the rollover: you are only allowed to rollover **tax-deferred** money into a traditional 401(k) plan. This means that if you have post-tax contributions in the previous IRA or 401(k) account (also known as tax basis) you cannot transfer those amounts into your 401(k) account. *(This situation provides the foundation for a RMD deferral strategy using an IRA and 401(k) account that we'll cover later in Chapter 19.)*

There is no annual limit to the amount of rollovers, and a rollover does not impact your ability to make your annually-limited regular contributions.

Designated Roth Accounts (Roth 401(k))

Another feature that many 401(k) plans offer these days is the Designated Roth Account, or DRAC. This is more commonly known as a Roth 401(k).

Roth 401(k) contributions are deferred from your paycheck just like regular 401(k) contributions, but you are taxed on the deferral as if you received it in income. This is the major difference between normal 401(k) contributions and Roth 401(k) contributions. You'll still be taxed on the deferred income when it is earned, however the growth of the contributions from investment returns is not taxed when later distributed in a qualified manner.

Roth 401(k) contributions can be matched by the employer, just like regular 401(k) contributions. If your employer offers matching funds and your contributions are Roth 401(k) contributions, the matching funds are placed in a tax-deferred (regular) 401(k) account. This is the same treatment as matching funds to the regular 401(k) account. So, if the only contributions you make from your salary are Roth 401(k) contributions, you'll also build up a regular 401(k) account if your employer offers matching funds.

Roth 401(k) contributions are limited by the same annual contribution limits as regular deferral contributions. In fact, the two types of contribution are combined together to determine total contribution for the year. The annual deferral limit ($20,500 for 2022 plus the $6,500 catchup) applies to the total of all personal contributions, but not to company matching funds. Company matching funds, added to your own deferrals, must be less than $61,000 (plus the $6,500 catchup if it applies) for 2022.

Distribution features/restrictions

The way funds can be distributed from your 401(k) account is yet another area where 401(k) plans can vary widely.

Some 401(k) plans allow for free distribution from the plan in any amount at any time after reaching age 59½ and leaving employment. Other plans allow for in-service distributions after reaching age 59½ - where you can rollover funds or otherwise take distributions while you're still employed. Some plans have an arbitrary "regular retirement age", which defaults at age 65.

Another option is to allow *only* a single lump-sum distribution from the plan prior to reaching age 72. This is an effort to keep the plan administrator's costs to a minimum, keeping the plan out of the business of maintaining distribution schemes for the participants. These plans must provide a method for administering Required Minimum Distributions to participants after age 72, but they may otherwise limit distributions to only single lump-sum distributions prior to that age.

RMD distributions

When a plan participant is no longer employed by the sponsoring employer and has reached age 72 (new as of 2020, used to be 70½), minimum distributions are required from the account each year. These are known as Required Minimum Distributions (RMDs). We'll cover RMDs in detail later in Chapter 19.

An exception to this rule is if the plan participant is still employed by that employer at age 72, then the RMDs are deferred. When the plan participant leaves employment the RMD will begin in the following year.

There is one exception to the RMD deferral past age 72 – if the plan participant is a 5% or greater owner of the sponsoring company, RMDs are required to begin at age 72 regardless of whether the participant is still actively employed.

§72t election (SOSEPP)

One more option for distribution of money from the 401(k) plan is to use exceptions listed in Internal Revenue Code §72(t). One of the exceptions noted in §72(t) is the ability to receive a Series of Substantially Equal Periodic Payments from the 401(k) plan (or SOSEPP).

A SOSEPP provides for a prescribed payment to the participant over a period of time that is the greater of 5 years or until the individual reaches 59½ years of age. We'll review SOSEPPs in detail later in Chapter 25.

Not all plans provide the option to set up a SOSEPP – specifically those that only allow a lump-sum distribution from the plan prior to RMD. In addition, a SOSEPP generally cannot be set up if the individual is still employed by the sponsoring employer.

Qualified Domestic Relations Order (QDRO)

Most plans provide a distribution in the event that a Qualified Domestic Relations Order (QDRO) is issued. A QDRO is a special court order as a part of a divorce settlement that requests distribution of a portion of an existing 401(k) plan to the ex-spouse of the participant.

An example is John and Judy's divorce. John has a 401(k) plan with a balance of $240,000. Among the other assets that the couple has, there are not enough liquid funds or other assets to provide an equitable split to Judy. The court issues a QDRO, requiring 50% of John's 401(k) to become Judy's property.

The 401(k) administrator will split the account into two accounts, one in John's name and one in Judy's name, with $120,000 in each account.

Unless Judy happens to be employed by the sponsoring employer, she will not be eligible to add funds to the account, but she can leave the account as is with the 401(k) administrator. She is treated the same as any former employee, with rights to distribution, rollover, NUA treatment, and other plan features. There is no tax implication to the QDRO split. Any distribution from Judy's account will be subject to ordinary income tax just like any other distribution.

Early distributions (after a QDRO split) are not subject to the 10% early distribution penalty, as long as the distribution is from the original 401(k) plan account established by the QDRO. If you have a QDRO 401(k) account and you rollover the money to an IRA or any other account (such as another employer's 401(k) plan), future distributions will no longer be eligible for the exception to the early distribution penalty.

5. The Best 401(k) Plan

With all of the features that are available in 401(k) plans, you have to believe that some of the features are more beneficial than others.

If you are evaluating potential employers, one thing that you should pay close attention to is the 401(k) plan and the features that are available in that plan versus other employers' plans. This is not to say that a 401(k) plan should be the most important factor when choosing between employers, but it should be at least one of the important factors.

Good 401(k) plans have low costs, well-diversified low-cost investment options, and no or very low barriers to participation. The plan should have flexibility in terms of allowing rollover contributions, along with a Roth option as well. A generous employer match, along with features to help you gradually increase your contribution level are important as well.

Put simply though, the very best 401(k) plan has a generous employer match and low fees. These two features alone count for very significant increases to participants' plans, when compared to plans that lag in either or both items.

The employer match is the easiest to understand. If this "free money" is significant, more employees will participate. Participating means you're taking advantage of the money that your employer is giving you, automatically increasing your investment, sometimes by more than 100%.

A typical employer match is 50% of all contributions up to 6% of employee compensation deferred. However, some companies take this to another level – I've seen plans where the employer match is as much as 7% for the first 6% of compensation deferred.

In such a plan, if your total income is $50,000 and you defer 6% ($3,000) to the 401(k) plan, the company will match your deferral with 7% of your compensation, or $3,500. So just by participating in the 401(k) plan, you've more than doubled your money. You gave up $3,000 in take-home pay (a bit less, by the way the taxes work), and the result is that your 401(k) has had a total of $6,500 contributed.

Naturally a plan with a very generous employer match will result in a much better overall result for the employee. Since each dollar contributed results in more than double added to the plan, over time this will be far superior to other plans.

Expense levels or costs within the plan are a bit harder to demonstrate, but this is the second most important factor to consider. Expenses cause a drag on the investment returns that your plan experiences. You may also see an item on your statement for administrative costs charged to your account if your employer passes these costs along to you as the participant.

For example, if your fund choices include two relatively similar large-cap stock funds, but Fund A has an expense ratio of 1% (often referred to as 100 basis points) while Fund B has an expense ratio of 0.3% (30 basis points), the resulting returns of Fund A will be 0.7% (70 basis points) less than Fund B, if all other things remain the same. Over time, Fund A will always lag Fund B, and compounding will eventually cause this difference to be very significant.

If both Fund A and Fund B experience an average return of 6% annually, on an initial $10,000 investment after 5 years Fund B has increased by 3.38% more than Fund A, a total of $431. Letting this play out for 10, 20, 30 years has an even greater impact, as you'll see in the table:

Year	Fund A	Fund B
1	$ 10,500	$ 10,570
2	$ 11,025	$ 11,172
3	$ 11,576	$ 11,809
4	$ 12,155	$ 12,482
5	$ 12,763	$ 13,194
6	$ 13,401	$ 13,946
7	$ 14,071	$ 14,741
8	$ 14,775	$ 15,581
9	$ 15,513	$ 16,469
10	$ 16,289	$ 17,408
11	$ 17,103	$ 18,400
12	$ 17,959	$ 19,449
13	$ 18,856	$ 20,558
14	$ 19,799	$ 21,730
15	$ 20,789	$ 22,968
16	$ 21,829	$ 24,277
17	$ 22,920	$ 25,661
18	$ 24,066	$ 27,124
19	$ 25,270	$ 28,670
20	$ 26,533	$ 30,304
21	$ 27,860	$ 32,031
22	$ 29,253	$ 33,857
23	$ 30,715	$ 35,787
24	$ 32,251	$ 37,827
25	$ 33,864	$ 39,983
26	$ 35,557	$ 42,262
27	$ 37,335	$ 44,671
28	$ 39,201	$ 47,217
29	$ 41,161	$ 49,909
30	$ 43,219	$ 52,753

By the time 30 years has passed, Fund B has outperformed Fund A by $9,534 – almost as much as the initial investment.

Although there are many other features that 401(k) plans can offer, these two features are the most significant in terms of the goal for the plan. Of course, the goal is to amass a substantial amount of money over your working career, such that you'll have an abundant source of income during your retirement. Adding as much money as you can, in the most efficient manner, while investing in vehicles with low expenses, will bring about this result much more quickly for you.

6. Defined Contribution vs Defined Benefit

Retirement plans are broadly categorized into two types: Defined Contribution (DC) and Defined Benefit (DB).

Defined Benefit plans are traditional pension plans. This is where the benefit amount has been pre-defined based upon the employee's service and compensation over time. An example pension calculation might be expressed as 2% times your years of employment times your final five years' average compensation.

So, if your average compensation in the last five years of employment was $50,000 and you worked for the company for 30 years, your pension would be calculated as

$$\$50,000 \times 2\% \times 30 = \$30,000$$

This type of retirement plan puts the risk on the employer – because it's a promise to pay a specified amount to the employee for the rest of his life (and to a surviving spouse if that option is chosen). The company must make appropriate investments to ensure that the pension will pay out as the promise is written. If there is a down year in the investment returns, they must make up the difference from previous years' surplus or make additional contributions to the plan.

On the other hand, Defined Contribution (DC) plans make no promise as to the amount of benefit that will eventually be available to the retiree. As the name implies, the amount contributed to the DC plan is a defined amount. This is determined by the participant in setting up the amount he or she will defer into the plan. Since only the contribution is defined, the investment results are not known in advance. This places the risk on the participant. If the investments chosen experience low returns or losses, the resulting balance upon retirement will be less than the participant anticipated. This can cause significant problems if the shortfall is more than the participant can manage.

Systematically, there has been a shift from Defined Benefit plans to Defined Contribution plans in the past 30 years or so. The switch from Defined Benefit plans to Defined Contribution plans occurred primarily to shift the costs and risks of retirement benefits from the employer to the employee.

This shift of risk has had a detrimental impact on the average worker in the US. Where before (with a DB plan) the worker could count on a specific amount of retirement income, now the future is uncertain. If the employee hasn't contributed enough and/or the investment results are poor, there may not be enough money to retire on. So, when the employee is ready to retire, he or she must make up the difference from another source, delay retirement, or learn to live with a lower income in retirement.

7. Withdrawals from your 401(k) plan

Once you've left the employer, you will want to take withdrawals from your 401(k). Depending on your plan's provisions, this can occur in several different ways.

If you're still a few years away from traditional retirement, you might want to rollover the money from the 401(k) plan into another deferred account. This could be to an IRA, another employer's 401(k), or other deferred account. This is known as a direct, or trustee-to-trustee, rollover.

In this case, you'd contact your 401(k) administrator and request a rollover of your funds from the current 401(k) account into the new account. There will be no tax or withholding on this rollover distribution, since you have not had control over the funds at any time and the money just went from one deferred account to another.

At the end of the tax year, your old 401(k) administrator will send you a Form 1099-R that details the distribution. This will be used to fill out your tax return for the year. Your new account will also generate a Form 5498 to indicate that the funds were deposited there.

A second way to transfer your money from the 401(k) plan to another deferred account such as an IRA is called an indirect rollover. To accomplish this, you would take a regular distribution from the account and then deposit the distribution into the new tax-deferred account within 60 days. As detailed below, 20% is withheld from regular distributions (by law), and so if you do not make up the 20% from another source in your indirect rollover, that 20% will be considered a taxable distribution.

Of the two rollover options (direct and indirect), the direct rollover is the preferred method. This is partly because of the 20% withholding requirement. But also, 60 days is a limitation that is set in stone, and if you miss the limit by even one day, the rollover may be disallowed. This would result in the full withdrawal being considered a taxable distribution, with significant costs in taxes and penalties.

A last way to withdraw money from the 401(k) plan is to simply receive money from the account as retirement income. If your plan allows it, you could set up a monthly distribution from the plan, in an amount that makes sense for your income needs. This would likely only be a viable option if you were over age 55 upon leaving the employer or over age 59½ if you left the employer earlier. Otherwise, you could be subjected to the 10% early withdrawal penalty. There are several other exceptions to the early withdrawal penalty. See Chapter 23 for more details on these exceptions.

Regular withdrawals are a simple matter to set up. You submit a request to the 401(k) administrator to send you a check for a specified amount. You can make the request one-time, annually, quarterly, or monthly, as your plan allows.

When the distribution is made, the 401(k) administrator is required by law to withhold 20% of the distribution for income tax. You will also have the option to have a percentage or flat amount of tax withheld for your state income taxes, if you wish.

You'll receive a Form 1099-R from the plan administrator after the end of the tax year, which will reflect the gross amount of your distributions. The form will indicate the amount of the distribution that is taxable, if you have non-deductible contributions commingled in your plan. Your withheld tax, both state and federal, will also be reflected on the 1099-R. You or your tax preparer will use the information on this form to prepare your income tax return.

8. Nondiscrimination Rules

There are certain rules, called nondiscrimination rules, that are applied to 401(k) plans. These rules are designed to ensure that the plan is used by employees at all levels of the sponsoring company, not just the highest-paid. *Note: as an employee/participant in the plan, you generally will not be involved with this testing, unless you're a highly-compensated employee. These rules are applied at the plan level, and the administrator of the plan takes care of the reporting and any necessary remediation actions.*

The nondiscrimination rules require that a specified percentage of all employees participate in the plan. In order to understand the rules, we must define a Highly Compensated Employee (HCE) first.

A Highly Compensated Employee is an employee who:

- Owned a 5% or greater interest in the business at any point in the tax year, regardless of compensation amount, or

- Received compensation in the amount of $135,000 (2021 income, applies to 2022 plan year) or more and is one of the top 20% of all of the company's employees ranked by compensation.

Once you have defined and identified the HCEs, everyone else is considered a non-highly compensated employee, or NHCE. There are three tests that must be passed to ensure that the plan is nondiscriminatory, and HCE and NHCE classifications are necessary to run the tests:

1. A coverage test, also known as the 410(b) test, from the IRC section which outlines the test. This test requires that the plan broadly covers all employees (HCE and NHCE) of the company.

2. Nondiscrimination of benefits (two tests, one of which must be passed):

    a. An Actual Deferral Percentage (ADP) test, comparing the average percentage of salary deferred by NHCEs to the average percentage of salary deferred by the HCEs.

    b. An Actual Contribution Percentage (ACP) test, which compares the percentage of all contributions (regular deferrals, after-tax deferrals and matching contributions) for NHCEs with HCEs.

3. A "top-heavy" test, which looks at the plan balances that have been accumulated by key employees. Key employees are different from HCEs – these are employees who are officers of the company, receiving compensation of $200,000 or more (2022 figure), or who were owners of more than 5% of the business, or who were owners of 1% or more of the

business and receiving compensation of $150,000 or more.

The first two tests must be passed annually based on the current or previous year's participation levels. The third must be passed annually but is based on the accumulated balances in the plan account. We'll review these tests individually next.

Coverage Test

The coverage test compares the percentage of eligible HCEs who are participating the in 401(k) plan with the percentage of eligible NHCEs that are participating. If the ratio of percentage of participating NHCEs to HCEs is at least 70%, then the plan passes the coverage test.

For example, Jenni's Widgets, Inc., has a 401(k) plan. Jenni has 3 other officers working for the corporation who are considered HCEs. All four of the HCEs (100%) are participating in the 401(k) plan.

There are 10 other employees (NHCEs) making widgets for the corporation. Of those, 4 employees have opted out of participating in the plan. That means only 60% of the eligible NHCEs are participating. The ratio of NHCE to HCE participating is therefore 60%, which is below the 70% floor (60% NHCEs / 100% HCEs).

When this ratio is too low, the plan benefits are considered – comparing the actual benefits received by HCEs to the benefits received by NHCEs for the plan year. If the ratio of benefits of NHCEs to HCEs is 70% or more, the coverage test is passed.

If neither of these tests is passed, there are a few corrective actions available to the plan administrator to bring the plan into compliance.

The first corrective action is to make retroactive contributions to all NHCEs so that the plan complies. Another way to bring the plan into compliance is to extend coverage to a broader group of NHCEs, perhaps by changing limitations based on employee classifications.

The second, often more severe, method is to require all HCEs to recognize and include in income enough previous vested benefits accrued under the plan such that the plan is once again in compliance.

Naturally the first option is the one chosen by most plans, as the second can cause an extreme tax burden for the HCEs, which presumably includes the owners of the company. There is no tax consequence to the NHCEs if the plan fails the coverage test, as long as the plan is remediated and brought into compliance.

Nondiscrimination of Benefits Tests

Under this category, there are two tests, one of which must be met on an annual basis:

Actual Deferral Percentage (ADP) – this test checks the percent of salary being deferred into the 401(k) plan by NHCEs versus HCEs. This test applies to both regular and Roth 401(k) deferrals.

The intent of the ADP is to ensure that all employees benefit from the plan. If HCEs are to maximize their deferrals into the plan, NHCEs must defer enough compensation into the plan to pass the test. This results in incentives from the company to encourage additional NHCE participation, often in the form of contributory matching by the company.

The ADP test fails if the actual deferral percentage of HCEs exceeds the greater of:

- 125% of the ADP of the NHCEs, or
- The lesser of:
    - 200% of the ADP of the NHCEs or
    - The ADP of the NHCEs plus 2%

The second test is the **Actual Contribution Percentage** (ACP) – in this test, all contributions, including deferrals and matching contributions, are compared between HCEs and NHCEs.

The point is to ensure that contributions (in total) are spread across both HCEs and NHCEs so that all levels of employees benefit from the plan.

The ACP test fails if the actual contribution percentage for eligible HCEs is greater than:

- 125% of the ACP for NHCEs or
- The lesser of:
    - 200% of the ACP of the NHCEs or
    - The ACP of the NHCEs plus 2%

The annual testing of ADP and ACP may be based on either current year figures or the prior year's figures. This choice is selected in the plan documentation.

Top heavy test

A third test (there's a third one?) is applied to determine if the plan is top heavy. This test looks at all accumulated balances by the key employees and compares the balance with the overall plan balance, including all non-key employees. If the key employee balances are 60% or more of the overall plan balance, the plan is top-heavy.

The first two tests review each year's deferral and contribution percentages. The third test looks at the accumulated balances of the plan. These tests must be checked within 2½ months of the plan year's end.

If one of the tests fails, corrective action must be implemented within 12 months, or the plan could lose its tax-qualified status. Losing tax-qualified status could result in severe tax consequences to all participants and the company.

Correction is accomplished by either making additional company contributions to the NHCE accounts or distributing excess contributions from the HCE accounts to the HCEs. The first method is more costly to the employing company, but the second method may result in a significant tax event for the individual HCEs.

Part 3: Benefits of 401(k) plan participation

9. Automated Savings

Participating in a 401(k) plan is an excellent way to automate your savings activities.

We all know saving money out of our paycheck can be difficult. There are so many things that we can spend our money on! From lattes and avocado toast to auto insurance and lessons on the clarinet, the possibilities are endless. Savings deposits are usually at the bottom of the list, if on the list at all.

By setting up a payroll-deducted salary deferral arrangement, your savings activity moves to nearly the top of the list. The savings deposit occurs before your paycheck is placed in your checking account, right after Social Security and Medicare tax is calculated, even before ordinary income tax withholding (if it's a regular, tax-deferred 401(k) contribution).

This way you don't have to decide between saving and other purchases – the saving activity occurs automatically for you.

Strategies for 401(k) participation

There are a couple of strategies that you could use to begin and gradually increase your participation in a

401(k) plan. These strategies work well to incrementally increase your longer-term deferrals into the plan, in a manner that makes it easier to acclimatize yourself to the reduction in your take-home pay.

The first option is to use the auto-increase feature (if your plan has this option). By using auto-increase, you might start by deferring 1% of your salary into the 401(k) plan. This small percentage should be relatively easy to live without in your month-to-month expenses.

After a year has passed and you've absorbed the 1% reduction into your spending plans, the auto-increase feature of the plan automatically increases your salary deferral to 2%. Again, this is only a 1% reduction (actually less, see the next section) from the take-home pay you've gotten used to over the past year, so you can likely get accustomed to this reduction quite readily.

Each succeeding year, an additional 1% is added to your salary deferral, and before you know it you're deferring a significant amount of your income to the 401(k) plan. (Studies indicate that 15% to 20% of income going to savings is a good target to aim for. The more the merrier!)

A second option is not as automatic, so you need to make these moves on your own. But this method is probably even easier on you than the auto-increase feature, because it's based on times when you receive an increase in your pay.

Benefits of 401(k) Participation

Let's say you have a pay increase of 2% coming to you. When that occurs, if you take half of the increase and defer it into your 401(k) plan, you'll still realize an increase in your take-home pay, while at the same time starting or increasing your 401(k) savings activities.

If you're a bit more hard-core about saving, defer the entire 2%. You'll still realize a slight increase in take-home pay (because of the tax deferral magic discussed next) while putting the entire increase into savings.

The magic of salary deferral taxation

The magical part of this saving is that, with regular (not Roth) 401(k) contributions, you're actually improving your economic circumstance by deferring salary.

For example, let's say your annual income is $40,000 and you're single. If you don't participate in a 401(k) plan, at the end of the year 2022 you'll owe tax on $27,050 (after your standard deduction of $12,950). The ordinary income tax on this amount is $3,040.50. Social Security tax (6.2%) on $40,000 is $2,480, and Medicare tax (1.45%) is an additional $580. Let's assume your state charges a flat 5% revenue tax as well to keep it simple ($2,000).

So, your net economic impact is your salary minus the taxes ($40,000 - $3,050.50 - $2,480 - $580 - $2,000), which equals $31,889.50. This is before you've done any saving.

However, if you participate in a 401(k) plan and defer 5% ($2,000) of your salary into the plan, the numbers change. Ordinary income tax will be based on $25,050, resulting in tax of $2,800.50. State revenue tax is reduced to $1,900. Social Security tax and Medicare tax remain the same, because these taxes are applied before the salary deferral.

Now your net economic impact is calculated by subtracting the taxes after salary deferral ($40,000 - $2,800.50 - $2,480 - $580 - $1,900) as $32,239.50. Of this, you've received $30,239.50 in take-home pay, and $2,000 is in your 401(k) account. By deferring 5% of your salary you've increased your economic benefit by roughly 1%, or $350. And this is before any company matching funds have been added to your account. We'll continue this example and look at the impact of matching in the next chapter.

Adjusting your contributions

Once you've started your contributions to your 401(k) plan, you have the option to adjust those contributions. Previously we talked about adjusting your initial contribution upward, so that eventually you'll get to a point of making maximum (for your situation) deferrals into the plan. But you can also adjust those contributions downward. Many plans allow regular adjustment to your contribution amounts, although some plans limit the timing of your adjustments to once annually or quarterly, for example.

Let's say you have a big expense facing you, such as replacing your home's roof. If your plan allows, you might suspend your 401(k) contributions for a few months, so that you can use the extra take-home pay to cover the roof replacement expense. After a few months, you can then adjust the contribution level back to where you were and continue with your savings contributions as before.

Most plans allow you to discontinue your deferral (stop contributing) at any time; however, you may have to wait until a plan entry date (often annually or quarterly) to start back up again.

Just remember to re-start the contributions! Otherwise you might get off track on your savings activity, and you'll need to go through the adjusting period that you went through when you first started the plan.

10. Employer Match

The truly wonderful part of 401(k) plan participation is the employer match.

Many employers match a certain percentage of their employees' deferrals into the 401(k) plan. This is done primarily to incent the employees to participate, at least up to a certain level. This incented participation helps an employer plan to meet the ADP and ACP tests that are required for a plan to maintain its tax-qualified status.

Employer matching is generally expressed as a portion of the first monies that the employee defers into the plan. Other times, there is a set percentage of employer contribution to the plan regardless of employee participation.

An example of employer matching is where the employer will match 50% of employee contributions up to the first 6% of deferrals. Continuing our example from the previous chapter…

If you've deferred 5% of your $40,000 income and your employer matches 50% up to the first 6%, this means an additional 2½% ($1,000) will be added to your 401(k) plan as the employer match. Now a total of $3,000 has been deferred into your account.

The economic impact of including your 401(k) participation is now $33,239.50 – as before, your take-home pay is $30,239.50, and now your 401(k) is $3,000. For your 5% income deferral, your take-home pay reduced by a total of $1,650 (from $31,889.50 to $30,239.50), but your overall economic benefit increased by $1,350. (As before, these calculations use 2022 tax tables and laws.)

If you don't participate by deferring funds into the 401(k) plan, you typically won't receive any employer matching funds at all. That is, unless your employer has implemented the safe-harbor option of making employer contributions for all employees regardless of participation level.

So, by not participating in a 401(k) plan you are actually leaving some of your hard-earned income on the table. The company is eager to give you this money — but you have to take the first step and participate in the 401(k) plan in order to receive it.

Beyond the matching of your own deferrals, sometimes employers make additional deposits to your 401(k) plan. One type of deposit is profit-sharing. When the company has significant profits from the prior year, often a decision is made by the management to share some of those profits with employees in the form of additional deposits to the 401(k) plan. These profit-sharing contributions are subject to the annual plan total contribution limitations mentioned earlier.

Another type of deposit that an employer may make to an employee-participant's account are corrective deposits (often referred to as Qualified Non-Elective Contributions, or QNEC) that are necessary to bring a plan into compliance with ADP and ACP discrimination testing.

When a plan doesn't meet one of the discrimination tests, often the corrective measure is to add more money to the Non-Highly Compensated Employees' (NHCEs) accounts, in order to bring up the percentages of NHCEs high enough to pass the tests.

This can also be done in reverse: in order to pass the ADP and ACP test, Highly Compensated Employee (HCE) deferrals might be distributed to the HCEs, bringing down the amount of HCE deferrals enough to pass the test. Distributions in this manner are subject to income taxation, but not early withdrawal penalties.

There are other types of deposits possible for your 401(k) account, most of which are limited in scope. These include true-up contributions (resulting from ACP and ADP testing) and settlement contributions, where applicable.

11. Vesting of Employer Match

Many times, an employer match is not immediately your own property if you were to leave the company. As an incentive for employees to remain employed by the employer, 401(k) plan documents often include a vesting schedule.

The vesting schedule determines the timeline, based on your employment at the company, for the matching money to be considered "yours to keep" when you leave the company.

Vesting refers to the process by which the employer-contributed amounts in the 401(k) plan become the unencumbered property of the employee-participant in the plan. Vesting is based upon the tenure of the participant as an employee of the employer-sponsor of the plan.

Generally, when an employee first begins a job there is a period of time when the employer wishes to protect itself against the new employee's leaving within a relatively short period of time. Vesting is one way that the employer can protect itself from handing over employer-matching funds from the 401(k) plan if the employee leaves the job very soon. Vesting can also apply to other employer-provided benefits such as a pension, profit-sharing plan, or stock purchase plan.

It is important to note that you are ALWAYS vested in the funds that you have deferred into the 401(k) plan from your regular wages and bonuses. Vesting refers solely to employer-provided contributions.

Vesting can be done in three ways: immediate, cliff, or graded. **Immediate vesting** is just as the name implies: the employee is 100% vested in employer-provided amounts immediately, with no limitations. In this case, if the employee leaves the company immediately after his or her first paycheck where 401(k) amounts were contributed on his or her behalf, those matching contributions are available to rollover into an IRA or other retirement plan, or simply withdrawn, right away.

Cliff vesting refers to a process where a specific period of time must pass, and after that the employee is 100% vested in the employer-contributed amounts. Until the specified time period has passed, the employee has a zero percent claim to the employer-contributed amounts in the plan. Federal law prescribes a 3-year limit on cliff vesting schedules for 401(k) plans. Any length of time less than or equal to 3 years can be a valid cliff vesting schedule.

For example, your company has a 3-year cliff vesting schedule, and you're participating in the 401(k) plan with company matching. If you find a new job and leave the company before you've been there for at least 3 years, you will forfeit the company matching funds that have been credited to your account, plus the growth on those matching contributions. If you wait until after your 3rd anniversary with the employer before you leave for another job, you will be allowed to access and withdraw or rollover the entire balance of your 401(k) plan, including the company matching funds.

Graded vesting is where a series of time periods pass, and after each of these periods a portion of the employer-contributed amounts in the 401(k) plan becomes the property of the employee. Gradually the employee gains more and more vesting (ownership) of the employer-contributed amounts, until finally the company matching funds are 100% vested.

An example of a 4-year graded vesting schedule would allow vesting of 25% per year at the end of each of the four years. After the end of the first year of employment, 25% of the employer-matching funds are vested. After two years, 50%; after three years, 75%; and after the fourth year the employer-matching funds are 100% vested with the employee. Federal law puts a limit of 6 years as the maximum number of years a vesting schedule can run.

So, if your company has a 4-year graded vesting schedule and you leave the employer after only being employed for 3 years, you will forfeit the remaining 25% of non-vested funds. The 75% vested amount will be available to you to withdraw or rollover as you wish.

12. Dollar-Cost Averaging

When you make regular investments of a set amount of money over a long period of time, you are said to be dollar-cost averaging your investments. With dollar-cost averaging, when the price fluctuates upward, you will be purchasing fewer shares of the investment, and when the price of your investment fluctuates downward, you're purchasing more shares.

Because of this, dollar-cost averaging can be an efficient method of making investment purchases. This is because your regular investment is in a fixed amount.

For example, let's say your regular contribution is $100 every week, and you invest this in a mutual fund. In week 1, the price of the mutual fund is $10, so you purchase 10 shares. In week 2, the price of the mutual fund has increased to $10.75, so you only purchase 9.3 shares. And so on, for several weeks. Listed below are the hypothetical purchases:

	Contribution	Price	Shares purchased	Total Shares	Investment balance
Week 1	$100	$10.00	10	10	$100.00
Week 2	$100	$10.75	9.3	19.3	$207.48
Week 3	$100	$9.89	10.11	29.41	$290.86
Week 4	$100	$9.20	10.87	40.28	$370.58
Week 5	$100	$12.48	8.01	48.29	$602.66
Week 6	$100	$11.57	8.64	56.93	$658.68
Week 7	$100	$12.07	8.29	65.22	$787.21
Week 8	$100	$10.88	9.19	74.41	$809.58
Week 9	$100	$9.79	10.21	84.62	$828.43
Week 10	$100	$11.40	8.77	93.39	$1,064.65
Week 11	$100	$9.78	10.22	103.61	$1,013.31
Week 12	$100	$11.29	8.86	112.47	$1,269.79
Week 13	$100	$8.50	11.76	124.23	$1,055.96
Week 14	$100	$10.54	9.49	133.72	$1,409.41
Week 15	$100	$12.00	8.33	142.05	$1,704.60
Total Invested:	$1,500	Average Cost:		$10.56	

As you can see, although the price has ranged from a low of $9.20 up to $12.48, your average cost works out to $10.56, due to dollar-cost averaging.

This process forces you to buy more shares at lower prices, and fewer shares at higher prices. Sound a little familiar? How about "buy low, sell high"? Even though you're not actually selling shares at this point, you're buying shares efficiently.

When you have small amounts to invest over a long period of time, dollar-cost averaging works much better than the alternative, which is to save up all of your contributions separately and invest all at once in a lump sum. From our hypothetical example above, if you instead saved up $500 at a time and indiscriminately purchased shares every 5th week, the results might look as follows:

	Contribution	Price	Shares purchased	Total Shares	Investment balance
Week 5	$500	$12.48	40.06	40.06	$499.95
Week 10	$500	$11.40	43.86	83.92	$956.69
Week 15	$500	$12.00	41.67	125.59	$1,507.08
Total Invested:	$1,500	**Average Cost:**		$11.94	

As it worked out, the average share price increased to $11.94, because the every 5th week purchases happened to fall on higher price fluctuations, compared to the 15-week example.

Note that this example was specifically designed to show this result, it could have happened that the 5th week each time was the lowest price point for the overall period, and so your average cost could have been lower. The point is that the more periods of time that you spread out your investment activity, the better chance you have of lowering your overall average share cost.

Plus, by investing the money as soon as you have it available to invest, you're taking advantage of another axiom: Success in investing comes from **time in** the market, not by **timing** the market.

In other words, by putting your money to work in your investments on a regular basis, you will have a greater chance of long-term investing success. This is opposed to market-timing, which is a process of guessing when the market has hit a low price (or trough) before investing your money, and then not purchasing again until another low price has been met.

Since stocks (on average) increase in value 3 out of every 4 years, targeting those low price troughs is difficult. And while you're waiting for a low price to occur, by sitting on the sidelines you're missing out on the upward-trending periods.

Putting money into the market as soon as you have it available works out far better than attempts to time the market in the long run.

13. 401(k) loans

An additional benefit which is exclusive the 401(k) plan (as opposed to an IRA) is that often 401(k) plans allow the participant to take out a loan from the account. There are restrictions on these loans, but generally a 401(k) loan is a much lower-cost alternative to a personal, unsecured loan.

Not all 401(k) plans permit loans, although most do. Much like many other features of 401(k) plans, loans are a possible feature, but they are not always a part of every plan. IRAs do not have a loan feature, there is no legal way to borrow a portion of your IRA or use the IRA as collateral for a loan.

Before we go into the specifics of taking a loan from your 401(k), since I'm a financial planner I have to put out a word of warning: Borrowing from your 401(k) should be considered a last resort option, when you've exhausted all other options. This is because when you take a loan from your 401(k) you are side-tracking a portion of your retirement savings due to the fact that you have to divert income toward paying back the loan. The end result is that instead of growing steadily via your payroll deductions, after the loan is paid back you'll be pretty much where you were before.

The good news is that taking a loan from your 401(k) may be one of the most cost-effective loans available, since you're effectively borrowing from yourself. The downside mentioned above should be factored into the cost, but if you're really up against the wall and have no other options, you can do much worse than a loan from your 401(k). Personal loans and credit cards typically have much higher interest rates (costs) as compared to a 401(k) loan.

Taking a loan from your 401(k)

Most 401(k) plans allow participants to take a loan against their account. (Some administrators restrict the option, so you'll want to check with the rules of your plan.) The way this works is that you determine the amount you want to borrow (there are limits, see below) and then submit the paperwork to the administrator to arrange the loan.

At the time of the loan, you also must arrange for the payback. Typically, this is handled the same way as your normal contributions to the account, via payroll deduction. There will be a particular interest rate applied to the loan, often tied to a rate index, such as "Prime plus 2%". This is generally a significantly lower interest rate than you can find in unsecured loan sources such as credit cards or personal loans. Home equity loans often have a comparable interest rate to a 401(k) loan.

Then your loan repayment period is set as well. The longest you can spread out your repayments is five years from the loan origination. You could choose a shorter period of time if you like and if your plan allows.

Benefits of 401(k) Participation

In addition, if you are unable to complete the loan repayment schedule as planned, you may have to recognize the loan withdrawal (or remaining balance) as a distribution, which is generally taxable income. If you're under age 59½ this could also result in a 10% penalty for early withdrawal, unless you meet one of the other early withdrawal criteria noted in Chapter 23.

Loan repayment may be suspended for up to one year in the event of the employee's taking a leave of absence, but the original loan repayment schedule will remain intact.

For example, if you take out a loan for $10,000 from your 401(k) plan, you might make a repayment schedule of 10 monthly payments. Each payment is $1,010, representing principal and interest. At the end of the 10 months, you have repaid your $10,000 plus $100 in interest, and all of this has been credited to your 401(k) plan account balance.

If you leave your employer, typically you are required to either pay off the loan completely or make a rollover contribution within 60 days to either the 401(k) plan or an IRA. This 60-day limit has recently changed with the passage of the Tax Cuts and Jobs Act of 2017 (TCJA), however. Now you have until the due date of your tax return for the year of the distribution to pay back the loan or complete the rollover.

For example, Willard has a loan with a balance of $10,000 against his 401(k) plan. He's been paying it back regularly, per the plan rules. In 2022 he leaves the job, but he doesn't have enough money to pay back the loan right away. His old job's 401(k) administrator considers this a distribution from the plan, and since Willard is 50 years old, there are no exceptions to apply. This will result in a 1099R at the end of the tax year from the 401(k) administrator, indicating a fully-taxable distribution with no exceptions applied.

In the olden days, Willard could still avoid the tax and 10% penalty on the distribution if he could somehow come up with $10,000 within 60 days after leaving the job and roll that money into an IRA. In the new world after TCJA, Willard doesn't have to come up with the money within 60 days: he has until April 15, 2023 to come up with $10,000 and roll that money into an IRA. This will avoid all tax and penalties on the rolled-over distribution.

Keep in mind that this only applies to 401(k) loan distributions that occur as a result of the employee terminating his employment or the company terminating the retirement plan. If the plan loan distribution occurs because the employee has not kept up with his payments against the loan, this is still considered a distribution subject to ordinary income tax and the 10% penalty if applicable. This type of distribution has no way to avoid the tax and penalty by way of a rollover.

If you are unable to pay off the loan, you will have to recognize the outstanding balance as a distribution as described above. The remaining balance is taxable as ordinary income, and if you're under age 59½ there will be a 10% penalty applied.

What are the limits?

I mentioned earlier that there are limits to the amount that you can borrow in a loan from your 401(k). The maximum amount that can be borrowed at any one time is the lesser of 50% of your vested account balance or $50,000. This means that if your 401(k) balance is $200,000, the most you can borrow at any one time is $50,000. On the other hand, if your account balance is $50,000, you can only borrow $25,000 (50%).

If your 401(k) balance is less than $20,000, you are permitted to take up to $10,000 or 100% of your vested 401(k) balance, whichever is less. So, if your vested account balance is $7,500, the most you could borrow is 100%, $7,500. On the other hand, if the account balance is $18,000, the most you could borrow would be $10,000.

Part 4: Roth 401(k) plan

14. Roth 401(k) plan Basics

More and more employers these days offer a Roth 401(k) option in addition to the standard 401(k). This option is a separate account from your standard 401(k), because it has a few characteristics that are different from the standard 401(k).

It should be understood that the Roth 401(k) is not actually a separate account (although you can think of it as such and I refer to it as such), but rather funds that have a designated source, identified as Roth contributions.

Roth 401(k) accounts are technically referred to as Designated Roth Accounts, or DRAC for short. This refers to the separately-designated account that houses your Roth 401(k) contributions and the growth on the investments that you make within the DRAC.

When you have a Roth 401(k), the process for participating is virtually the same as participating in a regular 401(k). Once you're eligible to participate, you sign on to the plan administrator's page and direct them to defer a portion (by percentage, usually) from your regular pay into the Roth 401(k).

Roth 401(k) contributions are treated differently from regular 401(k) contributions in that they are included in your taxable income *prior to* being deducted from your check. Whereas, regular 401(k) contributions are deducted from your taxable income in your paycheck and *then* taxes are applied afterwards when you withdraw. In both cases Social Security tax and Medicare tax are applied before the deduction of your contribution from your paycheck.

Other than the taxation differences – Roth 401(k) is taxed before deferral, while regular 401(k) is taxed upon distribution, plus the 5-year conversion rule (covered later) – in all other aspects a Roth 401(k) is identical to a regular 401(k).

Making the choice between 401(k) and Roth 401(k)

Now that you know the benefits of a Roth 401(k), you may wonder if a Roth 401(k) is right for your situation. This is not a simple answer, as with many investing and savings activities. It all depends on two primary factors: your applicable tax rate now, and your expectations about the tax rates in the future.

Your applicable tax rate now is important because if you choose a Roth 401(k) you'll be paying taxes on the income you are deferring into the account. On the other hand, if this same money was going into a traditional 401(k) account you would avoid tax on the money deferred.

So, if your current applicable tax rate is high, there is much value in deferring tax on some of your income. With a lower applicable tax rate, the benefit of deferring tax on contributions is reduced.

Looking into the future, if you anticipate that your tax rate in retirement is going to be lower than your tax rate today, then the traditional 401(k) is likely your best option. This is because you are deferring income at a high rate today and then later paying tax at a lower rate in the future.

On the other hand, if you anticipate higher taxes in the future (and let's face it, who doesn't?) then the Roth 401(k) might make more sense. This is due to the fact that by using the Roth 401(k) you can pay taxes today at your lower rate and then later withdraw those funds at a zero tax rate, when you expect that tax rates will be higher.

Pros of a Roth 401(k)

Among the positive aspects of a Roth 401(k) versus a regular 401(k) are:

- Future taxation is eliminated (for qualified purposes). Growth and contributions are tax-free when withdrawn after age 59½.

- Concerns over future tax rates are eliminated since you've already paid the tax on your contributions. If future tax rates are greater, you'll pay higher rates on regular 401(k) distributions – no tax is due on qualified Roth 401(k) distributions.

- Contributions could be withdrawn tax-free, with restrictions, prior to age 59½ – after you have left the employer.

Benefits of a Roth 401(k) versus a Roth IRA:

- Higher contribution amounts for the Roth 401(k) – up to $27,000 in 2022, versus $7,000 for a Roth IRA (catch-up contributions have been included, the maximums for 401(k) are $20,500 and $6,500 if under age 50).

- Employer matching contributions are available, although these must be directed to a regular 401(k) account, not the Roth 401(k) account.

- Income restrictions that are applied to Roth IRA contributions are eliminated with the Roth 401(k).

- Loans may be available against the balance in the Roth 401(k) account while still employed, if allowed by the plan administrator.

Cons of a Roth 401(k)

Negative aspects of a Roth 401(k) compared to a regular 401(k):

- You must pay tax on the income deferred into the Roth 401(k), whereas deferrals to a regular 401(k) are not subject to ordinary income tax.

- If tax rates are lower for you in retirement, you may have paid a higher rate on the contributions to the account, although the growth is still tax free for qualified withdrawals.

When comparing a Roth 401(k) to a Roth IRA, the following downsides are evident:

- Upon reaching age 72 your Roth 401(k) account will be subject to Required Minimum Distributions, just like a regular 401(k) or IRA. This can be mitigated by rolling over the Roth 401(k) to a Roth IRA upon leaving the employer.

- You generally* can't access the contributions to the Roth 401(k) before you leave employment, while you can always have access to the contributions to a Roth IRA account. (*Some employer plans have an in-plan distribution option, but this is somewhat rare, in my experience.)

Decision-point

The decision of whether to participate in a Roth 401(k) if your employer provides one is primarily the same as the decision-point of contributing to a Roth IRA versus a regular IRA. Actually, the decision between the two types of IRA is a bit more complicated due to restrictions on income levels and deductibility, which don't apply here. The primary questions that need to be asked are:

- Can you afford the tax on the contribution to a Roth 401(k) account?

- Do you think the tax rates will be higher or lower when you reach retirement age?

Affordability

If you can't afford to pay the additional tax on the deferred income (as compared to when you place the money in a regular 401(k)), then it would probably be better to choose the regular 401(k).

For example, if you're in the 24% tax bracket, deferring the maximum $27,000 into a regular 401(k) will reduce your taxes by up to $6,480. So, if you chose the Roth 401(k) instead, you'd have to pay that much more in tax. If this amount of additional tax will have a significant negative impact on being able to pay your day-to-day expenses, the Roth 401(k) is probably not a good option for you.

Keep in mind that the decision isn't all-or-nothing: you could choose to direct a portion of your deferral to Roth 401(k) and the remainder to the regular 401(k), which would allow you to manage the amount of extra tax that you pay.

Future Tax Rates

If you believe that the future tax rates will be greater than they are for you now, it may be to your advantage to use the Roth 401(k) – so that you pay tax at the lower rate now and avoid the future higher rate. On the other hand, if you believe that the rates will be lower for you in the future, deferring tax on regular (non-Roth) 401(k) contributions may be more to your advantage. Keep in mind that the current tax rate structure is scheduled to sunset in 2025.

Many participants choose the Roth 401(k) option simply because they are earning the income now, and they know that they can pay the tax. Whereas in the future, by having a sizeable Roth 401(k) to withdraw from, the individual can bypass tax at that time. By doing so, he or she has put the question of taxation (of at least this money) behind them, and they can focus on the future tax-free income instead.

15. Contributions to Roth 401(k) plan

When you make contributions to a Roth 401(k), the contributions are deducted from your paycheck, just like your standard 401(k) contributions. The difference is that Roth 401(k) contributions are subject to ordinary income taxes before the deduction occurs. Regular 401(k) contributions are deducted before ordinary income tax and are therefore deferred from taxation until distribution.

So, if you participate in a Roth 401(k), the taxation looks a bit different than with standard 401(k) contributions.

If you are single and your income is $40,000 per year, and you defer 5% ($2,000) into a Roth 401(k) account, your taxes on the income would look like this:

The ordinary income tax on this amount is $3,040.50. Social Security tax (6.2%) on $40,000 is $2,480, and Medicare tax (1.45%) is an additional $580. Let's assume your state charges a flat 5% revenue tax as well to keep it simple ($2,000). (These are 2022 figures.)

Your net economic impact is your salary minus the taxes ($40,000 - $3,040.50 - $2,480 - $580 - $2,000) which equals $31,899.50.

In-plan conversions

As of the beginning of 2013, a new provision became available for participants in 401(k) plans: the Roth

401(k) In-Plan Conversion. (403(b) and 457(b) deferred compensation retirement plans may also have this option available.) The in-plan conversion provision allows current employees participating in a traditional 401(k) plan to convert funds from that account into a Designated Roth Account (DRAC, or Roth 401(k) account) that is part of the plan.

This is new and different because previously the only way to convert funds from the 401(k) plan to a Roth-like account was to leave employment at the sponsoring employer, then convert the 401(k) money to a Roth IRA.

Plan administrators must amend their 401(k) plan documentation in order to provide for this provision. It's not a requirement, in other words. If your employer has amended the plan documents to allow for in-plan conversions, you may convert any or all vested funds from the traditional 401(k) plan into your Roth 401(k) plan.

This conversion is considered to be a withdrawal from the 401(k) plan, so ordinary income tax will be due for the amounts converted. You generally will not have access to plan funds to pay this tax. This means that you must have other funds available (non-401(k) money) to take care of paying the tax when you enact an in-plan conversion.

The amount of the withdrawal will be reported and included in your taxable income, added to your wages and other income for the year. Since our ordinary income tax rates are progressive, adding more income quite often results in increasing the tax rate applied to the converted funds.

For example, if you are single and your regular taxable income is $75,000, your marginal tax rate, meaning the rate at which your last dollar of income is taxed, is 22% (2022 tax tables). If you enacted an in-plan conversion of $25,000 from your 401(k) to your Roth 401(k), your taxable income is now $100,000. The marginal tax rate on this level of income is 24%. The action of the conversion has bumped you up to a new tax bracket, making the cost of the conversion more than you might have expected. The 24% rate is only applied to a portion of the conversion, that amount over $89,075 for 2022.

As we've discussed elsewhere, it generally only makes sense to convert money to Roth treatment if you believe that your future tax rates will be greater than your current tax rates. It is for this reason that the Roth In-Plan Conversion is often not a very attractive option, since while working you're probably at a higher tax bracket now than you might be later in retirement.

Keep in mind as well that Roth 401(k) funds are subject to required minimum distributions (RMDs) once the participant who has left employment reaches age 72, just like traditional 401(k) funds, but unlike the Roth IRA. RMD can be side-stepped for your Roth 401(k) if you rollover the funds from your Roth 401(k) account to a Roth IRA after you've left the employer. Roth IRAs do not require RMDs during the original owner's lifetime.

Situations Where a Roth In-Plan Conversion May Make Sense

Low income. If you have a relatively low income and have been participating in the 401(k) plan, it could make good sense to convert some or all of your 401(k) plan to Roth. This could come about if you have variable income (such as farm income or sales, for example) and you have a year where your expected taxable income will be lower by average than other years. Again, remember that you must have outside (non-401(k) account) funds available for paying the additional tax.

Estate Planning. If you don't expect to use the 401(k) funds for your own purposes in retirement and you'd like to pass along the money to your spouse or heirs, conversion to Roth will eliminate the tax burden for your beneficiaries. This could be accomplished by an in-plan conversion (while employed) or later by a regular Roth conversion after employment has ceased.

Higher tax rate expected. If you've read the tea leaves and believe that your future tax rates will be higher than at present, converting funds to the Roth could be a way to reduce your overall tax cost. In today's (2022) historically-low tax rate environment, it's not a stretch to imagine that tax rates will be on the rise in the future.

16. Company matching in a Roth 401(k) plan

If your company provides a matching contribution for your Roth 401(k) contributions, the matching funds are added to a *regular (pre-tax)* 401(k) account. So, if there is matching on your account, you'll have both a Roth 401(k) account and a regular 401(k) account. *As mentioned previously, these are really not separate accounts, but rather separate sources of funds.*

So, continuing the example, if your employer matches 50% of your contributions up to 6%, when you make the deferral of 5% to your Roth 401(k), your employer will make a matching contribution of 2.5% to your regular 401(k). At the end of the year, you will have contributed $2,000 to your Roth 401(k) and the company has contributed $1,000 to your regular 401(k).

Usually you have flexibility to invest your Roth 401(k) monies in any of the possible investment options, in the mix that you choose. However, some 401(k) administrators limit investment choices to a single allocation plan across all types of accounts – Roth 401(k) and regular 401(k). Check with your plan administrator for details.

You could defer some funds into the Roth 401(k) and some into a regular 401(k) account as well. The limit of contributions is based on the total of all deferrals, both Roth 401(k) and regular 401(k). The limit of deferrals for 2022 is $20,500, plus $6,500 "catch-up" contributions if you're over age 50.

For example, you may choose to break up your overall deferrals 50-50 into Roth 401(k) and regular 401(k). In the case of our example, this means you'd put 2.5% into the Roth 401(k) and 2.5% into the regular 401(k). At the end of the year you will have contributed $1,000 into the Roth 401(k) and the combination of your own deferrals and the company matching contributions will amount to $2,000.

You could also break it up so that you have exactly equal amounts going into each account, making adjustment for the company matching. In order to do this, you'd add up the total deferral percentages (5% of your own plus 2.5% in company matching funds, totaling 7.5%) and divide by 2. This gives you 3.75%, which you'd defer into your Roth 401(k). Subtracting 3.75% from your own total deferral of 5% leaves 1.25%, which is the amount you'd defer into your regular 401(k). At the end of the year you would have deferred $1,500 into the Roth 401(k). You've also deferred $500 into your regular 401(k), plus the company match of $1,000 for a total of $1,500 contribution to your regular 401(k).

17. Distributions from Roth 401(k) plan

When it comes time to take distributions from your Roth 401(k) funds, if you're over age 59½ there is no tax on the distribution, just like with a Roth IRA.

The difference (for distributions) between a Roth 401(k) and a Roth IRA is that you are subject to Required Minimum Distributions (RMD) from a Roth 401(k) account upon reaching age 72, unless you're still employed by that sponsoring employer. The RMD rules are the same as for a regular 401(k).

This RMD can by bypassed if you rollover the Roth 401(k) money into a Roth IRA. This is a straightforward transfer from one custodian to another (or it could be within the same custodian). The rollover is a non-taxable event.

Since Roth IRAs are not subject to RMDs, once you've rolled over your Roth 401(k) to a Roth IRA, the Roth 401(k) RMD rules no longer apply.

5-year rule for conversions

If you have converted money to a Roth 401(k), there is a 5-year limitation on withdrawal of the converted money from the account. The 5 years begins on January 1 of the year of the conversion.

If you converted other tax-deferred funds (regular 401(k) or traditional IRA, for example) into your Roth 401(k) account, you are restricted on withdrawal of the converted funds for five years after the conversion.

To illustrate: You converted $10,000 from your 401(k) into your Roth 401(k). The total Roth 401(k) account is made up of $70,000 of regular contributions, $10,000 from your conversion, and $20,000 from growth in the form of capital gains. Withdrawing $10,000 before five years has passed (if you're under age 59½) will result in a 10% penalty applied to $3,000 of the withdrawal. This is because withdrawals from your 401(k) (Roth or regular) are considered to be pro rata taken from contributions, conversions, and growth. Only $2,000 (the growth) would be subject to ordinary income tax, but the 10% penalty would apply to the $3,000 that represents the growth plus the conversion less than 5 years old.

In addition to the 5-year limitation on conversions, if you rollover funds from a Roth 401(k) into a new Roth IRA (you don't already have a Roth IRA in existence), there is a 5-year limit on withdrawals from that account. The 5 years begins on January 1 of the year of the rollover (when the Roth IRA was established). This applies unless you have another exception for withdrawal, such as reaching age 59½.

Part 5: Distributions from a 401(k) plan

18. Distributions at or after retirement age

When you leave your employer for retirement and you're at a any retirement age over 55*, you can take regular withdrawals from the account to use for day-to-day expenses. These withdrawals will be taxed as ordinary income – but no Social Security or Medicare tax will be applied. Depending upon your state, there may or may not be state income tax on your withdrawals from the 401(k) account.

*Age 55 is the earliest withdrawal age without penalty, but only if you left employment <u>at that employer</u> during or after your 55th year of age. If you leave the employer at any time before your 55th year, the no-penalty withdrawal age is 59½.

Some 401(k) plans have restrictions on withdrawals that occur before Required Minimum Distributions (RMDs) are necessary after the age of 72. In these plans, you may be limited to only one withdrawal per year, or possibly only one lump-sum withdrawal prior to age 72.

Generally, after age 72 there are no restrictions on regular withdrawals from your 401(k) plan.

When you take a completed (non-rollover) distribution from your 401(k) plan, the plan administrator is required to withhold 20% of the distribution for income taxes. This amount is reported on your year-end Form 1099-R and will be included among your other withheld tax and estimated tax payments for the year. Depending on your circumstances, the withheld money will either reduce the amount of tax that you owe, or increase the amount of your refund if you have one coming.

You can also rollover your 401(k) plan into an IRA or another employer plan. This is a straightforward trustee-to-trustee transfer, from your 401(k) custodian to another custodian. There is no tax consequence for a rollover, because all you've done is to move money from one tax-deferred account (the 401(k) plan) to another tax-deferred account (the IRA or other employer plan). There is no withholding (the 20% mentioned above) if you do this transfer directly between the two custodians.

If you rollover money from a 401(k) plan to an IRA, ERISA requires you to get sign-off from your spouse (if you are married) before completing the transaction. This is because ERISA provides certain spousal protections regarding your 401(k) plan, and when you move the money to an IRA those protections are removed.

A second method of rollover, known as an indirect rollover, may also be done with your 401(k) plan balance. With an indirect rollover, you request a

Distributions from 401(k)

distribution from your 401(k) plan and the administrator sends you a check. Within 60 days, you then contribute that money into the new account, whether an IRA, 401(k) or other.

Since an indirect rollover, from the point of view of the original custodian, is no different from a regular completed distribution, 20% is withheld from the check that you receive. If you only re-deposit the amount from the check (and not the withheld 20%), that 20% will be considered a completed distribution after 60 days, and you'll owe ordinary income tax on the distribution. If you're under age 59½ when this distribution occurs, you'll also be charged a 10% penalty on this amount, unless you meet one of the exceptions listed in Chapter 23.

For example, you have a 401(k) with a balance of $100,000 and you wish to do an indirect rollover to an IRA. You direct the 401(k) administrator to issue you a check for the balance of the account. Since the check is made out to you (instead of to another custodian) the administrator withholds 20% from the distribution, or $20,000. You receive a check for the balance, $80,000.

If you only deposit (within 60 days) the $80,000 check into your new account, you have effectively received a taxable distribution in the amount of $20,000. You could make up the withheld $20,000 from another source, such as personal funds, savings, or a loan. Depositing this additional amount would negate the

$20,000 withdrawal and make the overall transaction a tax-free event.

If you're under age 59½ when you do this indirect rollover and you don't complete the rollover with the full $100,000, you will not only owe tax on the distribution, but also a 10% penalty on any amount not rolled over.

Due to this 20% withholding problem (and the possible 10% penalty) it is generally recommended that you always do a direct rollover of 401(k) funds whenever possible.

You could also rollover your 401(k) plan to another employer's retirement plan – either at a new employer or an existing, older 401(k) plan from a former employer. This is subject to the receiving plan's administrative documents. Most plans these days allow rollovers from other retirement plans, but some do not. Check with your plan administrator to find out for sure.

The types of employer plans that you are allowed to rollover your 401(k) plan to include

- 401(k)
- 403(b)
- 457(b) (may require a separate account)
- SEP IRA

For these rollovers, there is no tax on the action of rolling over the money from one deferred retirement plan to another. That is, as long as it's a completed rollover, meaning all money withdrawn from the originating account is re-deposited into the recipient account (see the withholding problem previously in the discussion of indirect rollovers).

Another option is to convert all or a portion of your 401(k) plan to either a Roth IRA or a Roth 401(k) at a new employer. In this case, once again this can be a standardized trustee-to-trustee transfer, but you will be taxed on the amount converted to Roth treatment. This means that the amount converted to Roth will be considered a completed distribution from the deferred account, and as such ordinary income tax will apply to the distribution. Social Security and Medicare tax do not apply. You will pay this tax when you file your tax return at the end of the calendar year. No tax is paid on the actual date of the conversion, unless you do this by an indirect rollover (as reviewed above) and 20% is withheld.

19. Required Minimum Distributions (RMD)

Once you reach age 72, in most cases you will be required to start taking minimum distributions (RMDs) from your plan.

There is an exception to this rule: if you are still employed by the employer and you are a less than 5% owner of the company, you don't have to start RMDs at age 72. Once you do leave employment however, you'll be required to begin RMDs.

RMD and the 401(k)

Each and every 401(k) plan that you own, such as an account from a former employer, is treated as a separate account in the eyes of the IRS. As such, if you have four old 401(k) plans when you reach age 72, you will have to calculate and take a separate RMD from each 401(k) plan that you have.

In other words, you couldn't aggregate all the plans together and take one RMD from one of the accounts large enough to cover all the RMDs. In addition, you have to consider each account separately and figure out how much of each RMD is taxable, if you happen to have post-tax dollars in the account(s).

However, no matter how many IRAs that you have, the IRS looks at all of your IRAs as one single plan, so you are allowed to pool all of the account balances together, calculate the RMD amount, and then withdraw that amount from any single IRA account or any combination of accounts. Your tax basis is aggregated as well, so the tax treatment is a consideration for the entire pool of your IRAs in total (rather than account by account as is the case with 401(k) plans).

You have two old 401(k) plans and three IRAs. This is your year, you've reached age 72, so you have to start taking RMDs. How do you do it for these five accounts?

Each 401(k) plan's RMD has to be calculated separately – and the RMD taken directly from each account. But you can pool the IRA account balances together and take one RMD from one of the accounts that is large enough to cover all three accounts' minimum distribution.

This is another reason why it can be helpful (from a paperwork standpoint, if nothing else) to rollover your old 401(k) plans into IRAs. By doing this, you don't have to take a distribution from, in the case of the example above, three different accounts at a minimum.

Calculating RMDs

Regular RMDs (not from an inherited account) are based upon one of two tables that the IRS publishes. These tables are referred to as Table II and Table III (Table I is generally for inherited accounts).

Table III is the most common table. Users of this table are either single, married with a spouse who is less than 10 years younger, or are married with a spouse of any age who is not the sole beneficiary of the 401(k) account. If your spouse is more than 10 years younger and is the sole beneficiary of the 401(k), you will use IRS Table II. You can find these tables at www.IRS.gov in Publication 590, Appendix B.

To calculate the RMD, you need just two items:

1. Your balance in the account at the end of the prior year; and
2. Your age in the tax year of the distribution (as of the end of the year).

Go to whichever table (Table II or Table III) meets your situation and look up your age (for Table II you'll also need your spouse's age). Next to your age will be a Distribution Period. Divide your year-end balance by the Distribution Period factor. The resulting number will be your RMD for this year.

Each year your RMD will be different, because there will be a new year-end balance each year, as well as a new Distribution Period (because your age will have increased by 1). Run this calculation each year and you're all set. Just take the distribution before December 31 of the year. You'll owe ordinary income tax on the distribution, but there is a mandatory 20% withholding on your withdrawal (from a 401(k)) so you should have at least a portion of your tax burden accounted for.

For an individual who is 73 in the 2022, and the balance in her 401(k) plan was $104,804 at the end of the previous year, the calculation follows.

Looking at Table III, we find that the distribution period for age 73 is 26.5 years.

Now, we take the balance from last year's year-end statement ($104,804) and divide by the distribution period (24.7):

$$\$104{,}804 \,/\, 26.5 = \$3{,}954.87$$

This amount, $3,954.87, is required to be distributed from your 401(k) by December 31 of the current year. The distribution can be more, in fact I generally recommend rounding this amount up, in order to make sure there's no issues with rounding errors and it's clear that the distribution is adequate. In this case I would likely recommend a distribution of $4,000 to be safe.

RMD deadline

The operative date to begin RMDs is the date when you reach 72 years of age (this is new for 2020, in 2019 and before it was 70½). A normal RMD is required by December 31 of each year after you've reached 72.

When you first start RMDs, you're given a bit of a reprieve. Instead of being required to take your RMD by December 31 of that year, you are allowed to delay the first year's RMD until as late as April 1 of the following year.

For example, if you reached age 72 on May 11, 2022, your first RMD will is required in 2022. Your RMD for 2022 will be based on your 2021 year-end balance and your age in 2022. Calculate the RMD as described above.

Now you have a decision to make: you can either take the first RMD before the end of 2022, or delay to as late as April 1, 2023 for the distribution. Keep in mind, if you delay your first RMD to the following year, you'll still need to take another RMD (for 2023) by December 31, 2023 as well.

The reason that this provision was put in place is because often when a person is reaching the age to start RMDs, they also are leaving a job. Because of this, the individual's income in the following year might be significantly less than the year in which he or she was partially employed. This is a one-time option to defer the RMD income into the following year, and it might make a difference on your tax return.

The only time that April 1 of the following year is your RMD deadline is for the year that you reached age 72. For every other RMD year, the deadline is December 31 to take the distribution.

However, if you are still employed when you reach age 72, the year that you leave employment will be your starting RMD year, and you're allowed to delay that first RMD to April 1 of the following year as well.

Using 401(k) rules to avoid IRA RMD

There's a special strategy that you can use if the circumstances are just right. If you're over age 72 but you're still working at a company that provides a 401(k) that you're participating in, you do not have to take RMDs from the 401(k) account. You also must not have a 5% or greater ownership stake in the company that hosts your 401(k) plan to avoid RMD.

The special strategy comes into play if you have an IRA or other 401(k) from a previous employer that you're otherwise required to take RMDs from as of age 72. If your current (active) 401(k) plan allows rollovers of deferred money from outside the plan, placing this money from the IRA or old 401(k) in your active 401(k) account will effectively shield that money from RMDs. This will work up until you leave employment. Once you leave employment (and you're older than 72), you are required to begin RMDs. At that point, you'll also be free to rollover the entire account to an IRA or other qualified plan.

Qualified Charitable Distributions (QCDs)

When you are at least 70½ years old* you can opt to make distributions from your 401(k) or IRA directly to a qualified charity. The QCD distribution can also be used to satisfy your annual RMD if you wish.

This provision used to be tied to RMD age, but did not increase to 72 when the RMD age did.

This doesn't seem like such a big deal, does it? But the tax law has a nice surprise available if you use this option: the amount distributed as a QCD is never counted as taxable income on your tax return. So what?! you might say… who cares, I could make a charitable contribution and deduct it in my itemized deductions! No difference.

But that's where you're wrong. A QCD is not counted as taxable income (above the line, on the top of your 1040 form). The QCD is therefore not included in your Adjusted Gross Income (AGI, line 11 of your 1040). And keeping your AGI low is important for many other calculations on your tax return – such as medical expense deductions and many credits. Using the QCD keeps that money out of the equation altogether!

For example, let's say your overall income (including your RMD of $5,000) is $55,000. If you take the distribution directly in cash and then hand $2,500 over to your favorite charity, your taxable income will work out to $26,300 (subtracting the $25,900 standard deduction for 2022 and the extra deduction of $1,400 each for being over age 65 from your overall income). The key here is that your itemized deductions are not enough to be greater than the standard deduction. The level for itemization is especially harder to reach now that there is a limit of $10,000 on state and local tax, in addition to the fact that the standard deduction is a relatively high number, compared to the past.

However, if you made a QCD of $2,500 to your favorite charity and then took the remaining $2,500 as cash, your overall income for the year would only be

$52,500, since the QCD money isn't counted. End result is that your taxable income will now be $23,800 ($52,500 minus the standard deduction of $25,900 for 2022 and $1,400 apiece for being over age 65). You've satisfied your RMD, made the same amount of contribution to your favorite charity, and are paying less tax, because the standard deduction doesn't change. Big win!

The tax differential between the two strategies in our example works out to $300. Not a ton of money, but definitely money that you shouldn't just throw away.

Of course, the larger the QCD the better – if you qualify, you might want to consider making all of your charitable contributions in this manner. The limit for QCD treatment is $100,000 per person per year, so you have a lot of headroom to work with.

I believe this is a rare opportunity to take advantage of the tax law (after the changes in 2018), make significant donations to your chosen charity(ies), and pay less tax in the long run.

20. Distributions before retirement age

If you've left employment for any reason (other than retirement), you also have the options of rollover, conversion to Roth, or outright distribution.

The mechanics of a rollover were discussed previously – and as mentioned, the trustee-to-trustee transfer is the preferred method for doing a rollover. This is partly because of the 20% withholding issue (and the possible 10% penalty), and partly because 60 days can pass by before you know it. Missing the 60-day window on an indirect rollover is a final action, there's no way to avoid taxation and possible penalty on this completed distribution.

In addition to the rollover option, you can do a Roth conversion of your regular 401(k) funds. This is usually done via a trustee-to-trustee transfer as well. When you file your tax return at the end of the year, you'll owe ordinary income tax on the converted amount. There is no Social Security tax or Medicare tax on a Roth conversion. In addition, there is no 10% penalty on completed Roth conversions.

If you have funds in a Roth 401(k) or after-tax contributions to your regular 401(k), you can roll these over directly into a Roth IRA, with no tax consequences. This is not a conversion (as with regular, tax-deferred 401(k) funds going to a Roth IRA), so no taxes are owed when you roll over the

Roth 401(k) or after tax regular 401(k) contributions to a Roth IRA.

The last option that you have available to you is an outright withdrawal of money from the account. In doing so, you are not moving the money to a new tax-deferred account, but rather taking the money to do with as you wish.

Unless you meet one of the exceptions listed in Chapter 23, this sort of distribution can be the costliest of all. Of course, the distribution will be subject to ordinary income taxation, but you also may be assessed a 10% penalty for early withdrawal of your 401(k) funds.

For example, if you wanted to withdraw $10,000 from your old 401(k) plan at your previous employer, first off, the administrator will withhold $2,000 for taxes, and you'd receive a check for $8,000. But come tax time, you will have to include the full $10,000 as taxable income. You'll get to include the withheld $2,000 as withheld taxes, which might help with the tax bite, but the end result is that you have to pay tax on the withdrawal. In addition, if you don't meet one of the exceptions listed in Chapter 23, you'll be assessed a penalty of $1,000 (10%) on top of the tax.

If your money is in a Roth 401(k), you might think you could withdraw money from there without any tax, as you can with a Roth IRA. The reason this seems true is because distribution of Roth-qualified money, whether from a Roth IRA or a Roth 401(k), is never taxable to the extent of the contributions you've

Distributions from 401(k)

made to the account. Any growth that has occurred, either from capital gains, distributions of dividends, or interest, will be taxable if you withdraw these funds prior to age 59½, or prior to age 55 if you've left the employer at or after age 55.

This is one of the additional differences between a Roth 401(k) and a Roth IRA: distributions that are potentially taxable (prior to age 59½ or 55 as noted above). With a Roth IRA, your contributions are distributed first, followed by completed conversions, and then growth on the account (capital gains, dividends, interest). On the other hand, when you withdraw money from a Roth 401(k), each distribution is considered *pro rata* partly contributions, conversions, and growth on the contributions and conversions.

So, if you're under age 59½ and have a Roth IRA with $100,000 which represents $80,000 of contributions and $20,000 of growth or earnings on the contributed amounts, taking a withdrawal of $10,000 will be completely tax-free. This is because the first money withdrawn represents the contributions to the account, and you are free to withdraw your Roth IRA contributions tax-free at any time for any purpose. If you withdraw anything more than the $80,000 of regular contributions, the amount above $80,000 will be taxable as ordinary income. (Withdrawals after age 59½ are tax-free for both contributions and growth, although conversions less than 5 years old may be partly taxable.)

However, if you're under age 59½ and your $100,000 balance is in a Roth 401(k) (same mix, 80% contributions and 20% growth), when you withdraw $10,000 from the account, $8,000 will be representative of your contributions (and therefore tax-free), while $2,000 will be considered the growth, which is taxable. This is because every dollar that is withdrawn from the Roth 401(k) is pro rata considered partly contributions and partly growth on the contributions. In addition, if you're under age 59½ (or 55 if you left the employer at or after age 55) when you take this distribution, there will be a 10% penalty applied to the $2,000 that represents the growth in the account.

If you have converted funds from regular deferred accounts (401(k), IRA, or other) to a Roth 401(k) account, there is a five-year restriction on withdrawal of the converted money. If you withdraw money from the Roth 401(k) within five years after the conversion, the converted funds are subject to a 10% penalty unless you are over age 59½ (or another exception applies).

So, let's say the $100,000 in your Roth 401(k) account is made up of $10,000 of converted funds (less than 5 years ago), $70,000 in regular contributions, and $20,000 in growth. If you make a withdrawal of $10,000 before you are 59½, $8,000 will be tax-free (regular contributions and conversions) and $2,000 taxed as ordinary income (the capital gains). Furthermore, a total of $3,000 will be subject to the

10% early withdrawal penalty (the growth plus the converted funds).

21. Rollovers

After you've left employment, you are allowed to rollover the money from your 401(k) plan to an IRA or another tax-deferred account, such as a new employer's 401(k) plan. In some plans, there is an option to take an in-service distribution from the plan, rolling over a portion of your account to an outside account while you're still employed.

In many cases it makes a lot of sense to rollover your 401(k) to an IRA after you've left the employer. There are pros and cons to the concept of rollover, and often the balance comes down on the side of rolling over to an IRA. But you should consider the following pros and cons before you make that decision.

Cons (reasons to not rollover your 401(k) account)

1. If you are happy with your former employer's 401(k) plan, consider it well-managed, with low cost, and possibly with some investment options that are not readily available (such as desirable mutual funds that are closed to new investors), you may want to leave the plan right where it is. This is especially beneficial if you don't have another employer plan to rollover your 401(k) into, or if you are squeamish about setting up an IRA.

2. It is possible that maintaining a 401(k) account could garner you some employer-sponsored financial advice. Not all plans offer this, but if yours does, it could be a valuable option to keep. If you rollover your 401(k), this benefit would be gone.

3. If you have commingled deductible and non-deducted IRA contributions in your IRA account, having an active 401(k) plan can help you to separate the deductible IRA money from the non-deducted. Essentially this benefit gives you a way to bypass the "cream in the coffee" rule which requires you to aggregate all IRA funds pro rata when making distributions. This is a common issue when doing a Roth IRA conversion, for example. If you rollover your 401(k), this option may be lost, unless you rollover into a new 401(k).

4. If you have an investment in your former employer's stock in your 401(k), you need to consider the ramifications of utilizing the Net Unrealized Appreciation (NUA) option – before doing a rollover. Chapter 24 explains NUA in detail. One key point is, if you've taken even a partial rollover of your 401(k) in a previous year, the NUA treatment is no longer available to you.

5. If you think you may be returning to this employer, it might make sense to leave your funds where they are. This is especially true for

government employers with section 457(b) plans – due to the nature of these plans' ability to provide you with access to your retirement funds without penalty much earlier than an IRA or 401(k) can (see Chapter 28). With the vagaries of governmental policy changes, if you've withdrawn and closed your account and later come back to work for the same agency, the old plan may no longer be available to you since you're now a "new" participant.

6. If you're at or older than age 55 and are leaving the employer, maintaining the 401(k) plan gives you an option to take distributions prior to age 59½ without penalty. If you rollover your 401(k) to an IRA or to a new employer's 401(k) plan, this option is lost.

7. On the off-chance that you might need a loan from your retirement funds, you should know that IRAs do not have this provision. Retain at least some balance in the plan if you might need this option. Keeping in mind #5, if you've maintained a healthy balance in the plan and you return to work with this same employer, you'd have a much larger account to work with if you needed to borrow. Non-employees are generally not allowed to take a loan against a 401(k) plan.

8. Funds in a 401(k) account are protected by ERISA – and as such are generally not available to creditors in the event of a personal

bankruptcy. Depending upon the state you live in, IRA assets may be available to your creditors in the event of a bankruptcy. At any rate, ERISA protection is pretty much an absolute, so this is yet another reason you might consider leaving funds in a former employer's 401(k) plan.

9. Take your after-tax contributions out first, if your plan happens to include these. If you've made after-tax contributions, as some plans allow, it makes sense to separate these contributions from the pre-taxed amounts. You can then rollover this after-tax money directly to a Roth IRA in most cases without tax. This is because the 401(k) isn't subject to the "cream in the coffee" pro rata rule (as IRAs are) alluded to earlier, specifically for this purpose. Once you've removed the after-tax contributions and put them into a Roth IRA, you might want to rollover your 401(k) (the remaining money) to a traditional IRA if it makes sense.

Pros (reasons to rollover your 401(k) account)

1. You generally have more options available in an IRA as opposed to a 401(k). This is because most 401(k)s have a very limited group of investment choices – in an effort to simplify the offering so that participants are not overwhelmed by choices.

2. Better control of costs. Since you have (potentially) the entire marketplace of investments to choose from, you can choose the investment options that are lower in cost and are more effective than the 401(k) choices. Not all 401(k) plans have high-internal-cost structures, but many plans are more costly when compared to the options in the marketplace.

3. An IRA gives you the opportunity to take withdrawals at any point. Granted, you may owe a penalty on your withdrawal if there's not an applicable exception, but the comparison is that many 401(k) plans do not allow distribution (other than hardship) before you've left the employer. Additionally, after leaving the employer some plans limit distributions significantly, perhaps to only one lump sum distribution before your age 72. IRAs don't have that limitation.

4. Some early withdrawal penalty exceptions (see Chapter 23) only apply to IRAs. One example of an exception that only applies to IRAs is the first-time homebuyer exception. This exception allows the individual to withdraw up to $10,000 from an IRA without penalty to use in purchasing a home, subject to qualifications.

   Other examples of IRA-only exceptions include withdrawals for qualified higher education expenses, qualified reservist distributions, and payment of health insurance premiums while unemployed.

5. Some 401(k) plans do not allow the participant to choose the investment that you take your RMD from. In other words, all distributions come out pro rata from each the investments in the account. This might work well for you, but then again you might want to sell one particular investment and hold onto another. An IRA doesn't (generally) have that kind of restriction.

22. Taxes on your 401(k) plan withdrawal

If you take a withdrawal from your regular 401(k), you'll be taxed on the funds you withdraw. Depending on the circumstances, you may also be subject to a penalty. There's a lot of confusion about how the taxation works – and the taxation and penalties can be different depending upon the circumstances.

Taxation of the 401(k) Withdrawal

When you take a distribution of pre-tax money from a 401(k) plan, the amount of the 401(k) withdrawal that is pre-tax will be included in your income and will be taxed at your marginal income tax rate in that year.

Unless you meet one of the exceptions noted in the following chapter, your 401(k) withdrawal will also be subject to a 10% early withdrawal penalty.

For example – if you have a 401(k) plan at a former employer and you are 45 years old, unless your 401(k) withdrawal meets one of the exceptions in the next chapter, taxation would work like this for a $50,000 401(k) withdrawal (2019 tax rates):

Taxable Income before withdrawal	$60,000
Tax (assumes MFJ)	$4,780
Effective Tax Rate	7.97%
401k Withdrawal	$50,000
Other taxable income	$60,000
Total taxable income	$110,000
Tax (assumes MFJ)	$15,780
Effective Tax Rate	14.35%
Penalty (10%)	$5,000
Total Tax and Penalty	$20,780
Total Effective Tax Rate	18.89%

Nothing really dramatic about the first part, it's just more taxable income and you've likely grown to understand the effect of the graduated tax schedule. However, your 401(k) withdrawal of $50,000 resulted in $16,000 in additional taxes and penalties, or an effective tax rate of over 32% on the withdrawal. In the end you only net $34,000 from this withdrawal. Almost makes a payday loan look cheap by comparison.

The 10% penalty applies to the entire withdrawal amount, regardless of withholding (see later) unless your withdrawal meets one of the exceptions in Chapter 23.

On the other hand, if you met one of the exceptions (such as being age 59½ or older), the penalty would not apply. The effective tax rate on the 401(k) withdrawal is 10% less, at only 22%. The 401(k) withdrawal in this case only cost an additional $11,000 versus the income before the withdrawal.

Mandatory Withholding

Another thing you need to understand about your 401(k) withdrawal is mandatory withholding. Unless your 401(k) withdrawal is a direct rollover to another plan (such as an IRA), there is a requirement for the administrator to withhold 20% from the 401(k) withdrawal.

This 20% is sent to the IRS and will be included as part of your withholding and estimated tax payments that will apply against your tax when you file. If the withholding was too much, you'll get a refund of the extra withholding, just as you do from extra withholding or estimated payments.

Here's a continuation of the previous example to illustrate withholding:

401k Withdrawal	$50,000
Mandatory withholding (20%)	$10,000
Other withholding (W4 wages)	$7,000
Total withholding	$17,000
Total Tax and penalty	$20,780
Amount you owe	$3,780

As you can see, even though the mandatory withholding from the 401(k) withdrawal is substantial, it may not be enough in many cases to cover the tax and penalties from the withdrawal.

23. Early Distribution Penalty Exceptions

When hard times befall you, you may wonder if there is a way withdraw money from your 401(k) plan. In some cases, you can get to the funds via a hardship withdrawal, but if you're under age 59½ you will likely owe the 10% early withdrawal penalty. The exceptions listed below may in some cases apply to IRA withdrawals, but not all. Specifically, the QDRO option (#15 below) is only available to qualified retirement plans such as a 401(k). IRAs are not available for QDRO treatment.

Generally, it's difficult to withdraw money from your 401(k), especially while still employed. That's part of the value of a 401(k) plan – a sort of forced discipline that requires you to leave your savings alone until retirement or you'll face significant penalties. Many 401(k) plans have options available to get your hands on the money, but most have substantial qualifications that can be tough to meet.

Your withdrawal of money from the 401(k) plan will result in taxation of the withdrawal, and if you do not meet one of the exceptions, a penalty as well. See the previous chapter on taxes and your 401(k) withdrawal for more details about how income taxation works for a 401(k) withdrawal.

In addition to withdrawing money from a 401(k) plan, many plans offer the option to take a loan from your 401(k). This can be a better alternative than a withdrawal. A loan is often the only way you can access the money in a 401(k) if you're still employed by the same company. Chapter 25 explains the differences between a 401(k) loan and a 401(k) withdrawal.

The list below is not all-inclusive, and each 401(k) plan administrator may have different restrictions or may not allow the option at all.

Regular distributions

We'll start with the obvious methods, all of which generally require the plan participant to leave employment:

1. Normal – Begin after age 59½ after leaving employment at any age. This option may also allow for penalty-free in-service distributions from the plan. With an in-service distribution, you may be eligible to rollover or withdraw money from the 401(k) plan after age 59½ but before leaving employment. This can be a good option if your 401(k) plan has poor investment choices or high internal expenses.

2. Age 55 Exception – Begin after age 55, having left employment during (or after) the year in which you'll reach 55 years of age. This option is not available for in-service distributions – you must leave the employer to enact this exception. The key age is when you leave the employer.

For example, you might have left employment at age 53. After a couple of years, you want to take a withdrawal from your 401(k) account at the former employer. Since you left employment before the year that you reach age 55, even though you're 55 now, this exception does not apply to you. If you had waited until your 55th year to leave employment, you would still have this option available to you.

The Age 55 exception only applies to employer plans, such as a 401(k), and never to an IRA. If you've rolled over the money from the 401(k) plan to an IRA, this exception no longer applies, even though the money was otherwise eligible for the Age 55 exception treatment before the rollover.

There is a potential downside to this exception, in that many 401(k) plans have restrictions on withdrawals before age 72, RMD age. Some plans have these restrictions in place because they view the plan primarily as an accumulation activity, and they wish to limit administrative costs associated with managing variable periodic distributions. Not all plans have this restriction, but if yours does it could cause problems with your early distribution plan.

The problem comes about if you're planning to take (for example) monthly distributions from the plan from age 55 onward, and your find out that the plan only allows a one-time lump sum distribution prior to 72.

3. Age 50 Exception – Begin after age 50, having left employment during the year you reach age 50 or later, from a job in a public safety profession, such as police, firefighters or emergency medical services for a governmental unit. Only these specific professions are allowed to utilize the Age 50 Exception.

The same rules and downside apply to the Age 50 exception as apply to the Age 55 exception as noted above. Find out the restrictions on your plan before enacting a distribution under these exceptions.

4. Required Minimum Distributions (RMD) – technically this one is covered by #1 above for normal circumstances, but RMD is also required of a person who has inherited a 401(k), regardless of age. In all cases where RMDs are required there is no early distribution penalty.

5. Death – If you die, your beneficiaries are eligible to take distributions from your 401(k) without penalty. In fact, your beneficiaries are required to take minimum distributions from the account. See Chapter 30 for details on the treatment of an inherited 401(k) plan.

6. Disability – If you are "totally and permanently disabled" by IRS definition, you may be able to take distributions from your 401(k) without penalty. Total and permanent disability according to the IRS is a situation where both of the following apply: 1) the individual cannot engage in any substantial gainful activity because of a physical or mental condition; and 2) A physician determines that the disability has lasted or can be expected to last continuously for at least a year or can lead to death.

Now we'll move into some of the not-so-obvious methods, starting with SOSEPP.

Series of Substantially Equal Periodic Payments

This is the classic Internal Revenue Code Section 72(t) method for withdrawing funds without penalty. Essentially you agree to take a specified amount from your plan each year for the greater of five years or until you reach age 59½.

Once you begin a SOSEPP you are restricted to either continuing the payments in the prescribed amount (no more, no less) for the greater of five years or until you reach age 59½. Taking too much or too little from the account can cause dire tax consequences. See Chapter 25 for more details.

There are three methods of SOSEPP:

7. Required Minimum Distribution method – uses an IRS life expectancy table to determine your Equal Payments. There are three possible tables that could be used, depending on your circumstances: 1) the uniform life table (also known as Table III); 2) the single-life table (Table I); or 3) the joint-and last survivor life table (Table II).

The table that you choose will determine the amount of the distribution that you can take from your plan annually. The amount is redetermined annually based on your account balance at the end of the prior year and your attained age during the current year.

8. Fixed Amortization method – in this method, you calculate your Equal Payment based on one of three life expectancy tables (mentioned above). Then an amortization schedule is developed based on your life expectancy from the table chosen, and a rate of interest not more than 120% of the federal mid-term rate published by the IRS.

Once your dollar amount is determined under the fixed amortization method, that same dollar amount must be distributed in the subsequent years that the SOSEPP is in effect.

9. Fixed Annuitization method – this method uses an annuitization factor published by the IRS to determine your Equal Payments. With the annuitization factor, your account balance is used along with an interest rate not to exceed 120% of the federal mid-term rate published by the IRS. Just like the fixed amortization method, once your dollar amount is determined for the fixed annuitization method, the same dollar amount must be distributed each year while the SOSEPP is in effect.

See Chapter 25 for more details on SOSEPPs and how they work.

Other Section 72(t) exceptions

Section 72(t) provides several additional methods for taking distribution from your 401(k) which can occur before leaving employment (if the plan allows):

10. High Unreimbursed Medical Expenses – for yourself, your spouse, or your qualified dependent. If you face these expenses, you may be allowed to withdraw a limited amount (the actual expenses minus 7.5% of your AGI) without penalty. The expenses must be legitimate, paid medical expenses that are otherwise considered tax deductible medical expenses.

11. Corrective Distributions of Excess Contributions – under certain conditions, when excess contributions have been made to an account these can be returned without penalty. Growth on the excess contributions must also be distributed at this time. As long as the excess contributions and the growth are distributed before April 15 of the year after the year of the excess contributions, there is no penalty for this distribution.

12. IRS Levy – when the IRS levies an account for unpaid taxes and/or penalties, this distribution is generally not subject to penalty.

13. Qualified birth or adoption distribution – Up to $5,000 may be distributed to pay qualified expenses associated with a birth or adoption (new as of 2020). The withdrawal must be taken within one year of the birth or adoption.

Other non-Section 72(t) exceptions

And lastly, here are a few additional ways that you can withdraw your 401(k) funds without penalty:

14. Auto-Enrollment dis-enrollment – Within time limits, when you've been automatically enrolled in a 401(k) plan and you do not wish to be enrolled, permissive distributions may be allowed without penalty. Generally, this must be accomplished within a short period of time from the first contribution.

15. Qualified Reservist withdrawal – If you were called to armed forces duty as a qualified reservist after September 11, 2001 and served for at least 6 months, you may be allowed to make a withdrawal from your 401(k) *during your active duty period* without penalty.

16. Divorce QDRO – If a Qualified Domestic Relations Order (QDRO) is issued as part of a divorce decree with the order to assign or divide and assign a portion of the assets of your 401(k) plan to your former spouse, this withdrawal is penalty-free. As long as the money remains in the partitioned account that results from the QDRO, the receiving party can take distributions from the account without penalty. This treatment is lost if the QDRO portion of the account is rolled over into an IRA or another employer plan.

As an example, let's say Lester and Edwina (both age 40) are divorcing. As a part of the divorce settlement, Edwina's 401(k) plan is to be shared with Lester, 50/50, with a QDRO enforcing the split. After a couple of years Lester decides he would like to use some of the funds awarded to him from the divorce to purchase a new fishing boat. As long as the funds are still held in the 401(k) plan, Lester can request withdrawal and receive the funds without penalty, due to the existence of the QDRO. However, had Lester rolled over the funds into an IRA (or other qualified plan), the QDRO would no longer be in effect, and he would be unable to access the funds without paying the penalty for early withdrawal. (It is important to note that, in either case, Lester would be required to pay ordinary income tax on the distribution.)

17. Roth IRA or Roth 401(k) Conversion – when you convert your funds from a 401(k) plan to a Roth IRA or Roth 401(k), although you pay tax on the distribution, there is no 10% penalty applied to the converted amount. Usually you must have left employment to enact a conversion to Roth IRA. Many employers allow in-service conversions to a Roth 401(k) within the same plan with no penalty.

18. Pass-through dividend from ESOP - if your plan includes an ESOP (Employee Stock Ownership Plan), dividends from the stock can be passed through to you personally without penalty.

24. Net Unrealized Appreciation (NUA)

This widely misunderstood section of the IRS code can be quite a benefit – if it happens to fit your situation. Net Unrealized Appreciation (NUA) refers to the increase in value of your company's stock held within your 401(k), due to your own investment in the company stock within the 401(k). Other company-sponsored deferred accounts can apply here as well, but the primary type of account is the 401(k), so we'll refer to all company-sponsored tax-deferred accounts as 401(k)'s for the purpose of this discussion.

In order to take advantage of the Net Unrealized Appreciation provision, first of all you must hold your company's stock in your 401(k) or other deferred taxation plan, and you must be in a position to roll over the account. That is, either you must have separated from service by leaving employment (voluntarily or involuntarily), or the 401(k) plan is being terminated.

As you consider the rollover of your funds, if the company stock has increased in value, you have net unrealized appreciation. That is, there is a net increase or appreciation in value that has not yet been realized by sale of the stock. The IRS allows for this net unrealized appreciation to be treated as a capital gain, which can result in much lower tax rates on the gain versus ordinary income tax rates.

In order to take advantage of this special NUA treatment, the 401(k) account must be completely distributed in one tax year. There is one thing that you must do differently from other rollovers, however: The company stock will be rolled over into a taxable (non-IRA) account, while everything else will be rolled over into a traditional IRA, or possibly distributed as cash.

When you rollover the company stock, this will be considered a distribution. As with any distribution, you will be required to pay the tax. However, in the NUA treatment, you are only required to pay tax on the basis (original cost) of the stock, but not on the appreciation or growth in value of the stock. You may also have to pay the 10% penalty (on the basis) if you were under age 55 when you left the employer and under age 59½ when you take the distribution. Your employer or plan administrator will have records on your basis of the stock.

As an example, let's say Frank has participated in the company's 401(k) plan for several years and he's now ready to retire. Part of the 401(k) funds were invested over the years in Frank's company's stock, which has cost Frank a total of $10,000 through the years (this is the basis). Frank's company has done well, and now the stock is worth $150,000 in the market. If Frank rolled over the company stock into an IRA, when he withdraws the money he would pay ordinary income tax on the entire amount of $150,000 — at whatever his current marginal income tax rate at that time. Instead of going that route, Frank decides to use the

NUA provision in the tax law – much to his advantage.

Frank sets up an IRA and a taxable account at the custodian of his choice, and he directs the 401(k) administrator to distribute his company stock to the taxable account, and rollover all other funds from the 401(k) to the IRA. When Frank moves the company stock into the taxable account, he will be taxed at ordinary income tax rates (plus the 10% penalty if he was under age 59½) on the basis of the stock – which is $10,000. Now, not only will the growth of the stock ($140,000) have a tax rate of 20% or less as capital gains, Frank also will not have to take required minimum distributions (RMD) from those funds upon reaching age 72. Frank can leave the company stock in that taxable account for the rest of his life if he wishes, and then hand it over to his heirs. (Note: NUA stock doesn't receive a step-up in basis when passed to heirs like other appreciated stock.)

Here's the math: Frank pays tax at an example rate of 25% on the $10,000 basis of the stock, or $2,500. Frank is over age 59½, so no 10% penalty applies. Then, as he sells the stock, the total amount of capital gains tax would be at a maximum 20% at today's rates on $140,000 (just the growth!) or a total of $28,000. Depending on Frank's income level when he sells the stock, the capital gains tax could be 15% or even zero. Compare that to the non-NUA treatment, where Frank would be taxed with ordinary income tax rates on the entire $150,000 stock value over time, for a total of $37,500 at the 25% rate! In this example, at a minimum Frank has saved a total of $9,500 in taxes!

Now, NUA treatment doesn't work for all situations. For example, if your company stock has only grown minimally in value, or has gone down in value, there is little or no benefit to utilizing the NUA option. Also, if the basis of the stock is fairly high relative to the growth, it might make sense to only apply NUA treatment to a portion of your company stock, which is also allowed. One last thing – this NUA treatment only applies to the stock of your employer. No other stock can receive this treatment.

Which company stock can be treated with NUA?

Not all of the company stock in your account is available for NUA treatment. This is where we'll define what cannot be treated in that fashion. The following items cannot be used for NUA, and they make up the **basis** of the company stock in your account:

- Your contributions to the plan that are attributable to the employer stock

- Your employer's contributions to the plan, attributable to the employer stock

- The Net Unrealized Appreciation in the stock attributed to employer contributions

Those three items will be taxed as ordinary income in the year that the distribution occurred. So, the only thing that is left, Net Unrealized Appreciation of the company stock purchased with your own contributions, can be taxed with capital gains tax – instead of ordinary income tax, as all other pre-tax distributions from the plan are treated.

This is not an all-or-nothing provision. You have the option to elect NUA treatment for only a portion of your overall distribution from the account. Everything else could be rolled over into another employer plan or an IRA, further deferring taxation.

Holding period

The stock distributed from the employer plan that you've elected to use NUA treatment on is treated as having been held for greater than one year. Therefore, the growth that is distributed (the NUA) will have the characteristic of long-term capital gains tax treatment. Additional gains beyond the initial NUA have a holding period that begins with the date of distribution – so when you sell the stock, some of your gains could be short-term or long-term capital gains, depending on when you take the distribution.

25. 72(t) SOSEPP Distributions

As mentioned briefly in Chapter 23, three of the exceptions to the early withdrawal penalty are known as SOSEPP, which stands for Series of Substantially Equal Periodic Payments. This is also often referred to as 72(t) payments, since that is the Internal Revenue Code section that describes this and several other, lesser-known, exceptions to the early distribution penalty.

This particular section of the Internal Revenue Code – specifically §72(t)(2)(A)(iv) – is the most famous of the 72(t) provisions. This is mostly due to the fact that it seems to be the ultimate answer to the age-old question "How can I take money out of my IRA or 401(k) without penalty?"

While it's true that this particular code section provides a method for getting at your retirement funds without penalty (and without special circumstances like medical issues), this code section is very complicated. With this complication comes a huge potential for costly mistakes – and the IRS does NOT forgive and forget!

A Series of Substantially Equal Periodic Payments, or SOSEPP is just what it sounds like. You withdraw a specified amount from your IRA or 401(k) every year. The specified amount is not always the same (hence "substantially" equal) but the method for determining the amount is the same year after year. You start your

SOSEPP at some age before 59½ years of age, and you must continue those payments for the greater of 5 years or until you reach age 59½.

In order to set up your Series of Substantially Equal Periodic Payments (SOSEPP), you must use one of the three methods prescribed by the IRS: Required Minimum Distribution method, Fixed Amortization method, and Fixed Annuitization method (more information on each method follows later in this chapter).

Once chosen, your method cannot be changed under most circumstances. There is one situation that provides for a one-time change to your payments (see One-time change to SOSEPP, later), but otherwise the SOSEPP can't be changed without "busting" the strategy. This means that every year the SOSEPP is in effect, you must take exactly the amount in your schedule from your retirement account, no more and no less. Making a change to your withdrawal schedule will result in your owing the 10% penalty retroactively on all payments received to that point, plus interest.

In addition, once you've begun your SOSEPP, you must continue that payment schedule until the later of five years or you reach age 59½. Again, this is an area where the IRS doesn't forgive or give any leeway: if you take additional distributions one day before your five years or your age 59½, the action will "bust" the SOSEPP, and you'll be liable for 10% penalty on all distributions from your 401(k) plus interest. Obviously, this sort of an arrangement should not be taken lightly, and you must keep excellent, flawless records of your withdrawals.

Other facts about SOSEPP:

- Before you start your SOSEPP, you can split your IRA into more than one account, and then apply your SOSEPP against only one account, thereby reducing the balance against which your payout method is calculated. This splitting typically is not available for a 401(k) plan, although you could rollover a portion of the 401(k) to an IRA and use a SOSEPP against either account, as long as the plan administrator allows.

- You can have more than one SOSEPP going at a time, using separate IRA or 401(k) accounts and different payout methods for each. This might help to customize your payments.

- Your periodic payment will likely change under the minimum distribution method, as it recalculates annually based on the account balance at the end of the prior year. The other two methods typically do not change payment amounts over time.

Required Minimum Distribution Method

The Required Minimum Distribution method for calculating your SOSEPP determines a specific amount that you must withdraw from your IRA, 401k, or other retirement plan each year, based upon your account balance at the end of the previous year. The balance is then divided by the life expectancy factor from either the Single Life Expectancy table (Table I) or the Joint Life and Last Survivor Expectancy table (Table II), using the age(s) you have reached (or will reach) by the end of the current calendar year. This annual amount will be different each year, since the balance at the end of the previous year will be different, and your age factor will be different as well.

Which table you use is based upon your circumstances. If you are single, or married with a spouse who is less than 10 years younger than you, you will use the Single Life Expectancy table. If you are married and your spouse is 10 years or more younger, you may choose to use the Joint Life and Last Survivor Expectancy table. These tables are available at www.IRS.gov, Publication 590.

Fixed Amortization Method

When calculating your SOSEPP, a second choice is the Fixed Amortization method.

Calculating your annual payment under this method requires you to have the balance of your IRA account when starting the SOSEPP. With this balance you then create an amortization schedule over a specified number of years equal to your life expectancy factor from either the Single Life Expectancy table (Table I) or the Joint Life and Last Survivor Expectancy table (Table II), using the age you have reached (or will reach) for that calendar year. The amortization table must use a rate of interest of your choice, but the chosen rate cannot be more than 120% of the federal mid-term rate published regularly by the IRS in an Internal Revenue Bulletin (IRB).

Which table you use is based upon your circumstances. If you are single, or married with a spouse who is less than 10 years younger than you, you will use the Single Life Expectancy table. If you are married and your spouse is 10 years or more younger, you may choose to use the Joint Life and Last Survivor Expectancy table.

Once you've calculated your annual payment under the Fixed Amortization method, your future payments will be exactly the same until the SOSEPP is no longer in effect. There is a one-time opportunity to change to the Required Minimum Distribution method. This one-time change is detailed a bit later in this chapter.

Fixed Annuitization Method

The third and final option for determining the amount of your SOSEPP is the Fixed Annuitization method.

Calculating your annual payment under this method requires you to have the balance of your IRA or 401(k) account and an annuity factor, which is found in Appendix B of Rev. Ruling 2002-62 using the age you have reached (or will reach) for that calendar year. You will then specify a rate of interest of your choice that is not more than 120% of the federal mid-term rate published regularly by the IRS in an Internal Revenue Bulletin (IRB).

Once you've calculated your annual payment under the Fixed Annuitization method, your future payments will be exactly the same until the SOSEPP is no longer in effect. Just like the Fixed Amortization Method, there is a one-time opportunity to change to the Required Minimum Distribution method, which we'll cover next.

One-time change to SOSEPP

Generally, when you establish a SOSEPP you have to stick with your plan for the longer of five years or until you reach age 59½. However, the IRS allows changing your SOSEPP one time, and only one time. And then, the rules only allow changing your SOSEPP from either the Fixed Annuitization method or the Fixed Amortization method to the Required Minimum Distribution method.

This is the only exception allowed for changing your SOSEPP during its enforcement period, which is the later of five years after you started the SOSEPP or when you turn age 59½. The exception is documented in Rev. Ruling 2002-62, 2.03(b).

If you're planning on changing your SOSEPP in a manner other than the above-described methods, you will effectively "bust" the plan, meaning that the SOSEPP is no longer in place. Doesn't sound like such a bad thing, right? That's where you're wrong though… because if you bust a SOSEPP, there are some very nasty ways that the IRS will get back at you.

Busting the plan can be as simple as increasing or decreasing the amount you withdraw slightly, or forgetting to make a withdrawal altogether, or possibly taking two distributions (a double-dip) in one year. There's no room for "forgive and forget" on this from the IRS. For more on the consequences of busting a SOSEPP, see the next section.

There is no specific provision in the Internal Revenue Code for relief from the penalty if you have busted your SOSEPP. On the other hand, the IRS has in some cases granted relief in several private letter rulings by determining that a change in the series of payments did not materially modify the series for purposes of the rules.

If the series is busted due to an error by an advisor (for example), some prior PLRs have been issued in favor of the taxpayer. PLR 201051025 and PLR 200503036 each address the situation of an advisor making an error and the distributions were allowed to be made up in the subsequent year. **Bear in mind that PLRs are not valid for any other circumstances other than the specific one in the ruling, and cannot be used to establish precedence for subsequent cases.**

In reality, the likelihood of your getting a favorable PLR for your case of a busted SOSEPP is small – unfortunately, busting the series usually results in application of the penalty for previous payments received, and the SOSEPP is eliminated. If you wish to restart the series you can do so, but you are starting with a new five-year timeline (the series must exist for at least five years, or until you reach age 59½, whichever is later).

Penalties for busting a SOSEPP

What happens if you make a change to your distributions while subject to a SOSEPP? Other than the one-time change discussed previously, you were supposed to keep the same payment for the longer of 5 years or until age 59½. What do you do now?

Well – first of all, we must understand the timeline associated with a SOSEPP: once begun (notwithstanding the "one-time change" exception), you have to continue those periodic payments without change for the longer of five years or until you reach age 59½.

If you make a change to your periodic payments (other than the one-time change), IRC §72(t)(4) indicates that ALL of your payments, beginning with your first payment under the SOSEPP, will be subject to 1) ordinary income tax (should have already been assessed); 2) the 10% non-qualified withdrawal penalty; and 3) interest on any unpaid tax or penalty, calculated from the date(s) of the disbursal(s) forward to the date you busted the SOSEPP.

This Code section should strike fear in the hearts of folks who are considering a SOSEPP. If you think about it, the possibilities for error are numerous. Your brokerage can fail to execute a disbursement the way you directed; you forget to take your withdrawal; you mistakenly take more (or less) than your SOSEPP prescribes… And if it's been in place for several years, you'll owe penalties back to the beginning of the plan, plus interest.

It doesn't take much imagination to envision a scenario where you could be in pretty deep with such an error on your plan. The IRS has no sense of humor when dealing with these cases – not many are overturned.

26. 401(k) loan versus withdrawal

When you have a 401(k) and you need some money from the account, you have a couple of options. Depending upon your 401(k) plan's features, you may be able to take a 401(k) loan. With some plans you also have the option to take an early, in-service withdrawal from the plan.

These two options have very different outcomes for you, in terms of taxes and possible penalties. Let's explore the differences.

401(k) Loan

If your plan allows for a 401(k) loan, this can be a good option to get access to the money, for virtually any purpose. Being a loan, there is no tax impact when you take out the loan. Plus, you can use the money for any purpose that you need, at any age.

However, as a loan it must be paid back over a five-year period (at most). You'll pay interest on the loan, but since it is from your own account, you're paying interest to yourself.

There is a limit of $50,000 for a 401(k) loan, or 50% of your account balance if that amount is less. If your account balance is less than $20,000, you are allowed to take up to the lesser of $10,000 or your full account balance in a loan.

If you leave the employer (for retirement or otherwise) and there is still a balance outstanding on your 401(k) loan, the outstanding balance will be considered a withdrawal from the 401(k) account unless you pay it back. If you don't pay it back, the withdrawal is taxable as ordinary income and possibly subject to the 10% early withdrawal penalty (unless you meet one of the exceptions, see Chapter 23).

You have the option of repaying the loan in full before your tax return is due for the year (April 15 of the following year). If you do so, the outstanding loan will no longer be considered a taxable distribution. You also have the option of completing a rollover of your outstanding balance into an IRA. You would do this by contributing an amount equal to the outstanding loan balance to an IRA prior to April 15 of the following year.

If you are not currently employed by the sponsoring employer, a 401(k) loan is generally not available.

401(k) Withdrawal

If you're still employed by the company and want to take a withdrawal from your 401(k), the 401(k) plan must have an option to allow for in-service withdrawals. Often there are restrictions on the availability of an in-service withdrawal. For many plans it's necessary to be above a certain age (such as 59½ years of age), or that a particular requirement is met, such as hardship by the employee, defined by the plan administrator.

In addition, if you're taking a withdrawal from the plan instead of a 401(k) loan, the money withdrawn

Distributions from 401(k)

from the 401(k) plan will be taxable to you as ordinary income. Plus, if you're under age 59½ your withdrawal could be subject to an early withdrawal penalty unless you meet one of the exceptions. See Chapter 23 for the exceptions to the 10% penalty.

The good news is that you won't have to pay the money back to the plan when you make a withdrawal as you would with a 401(k) loan. However, by taking a withdrawal, you have permanently removed that money from your retirement savings process, which will ultimately reduce the amount of money you'll have when you reach retirement age.

Part 6: Other employer retirement plans

In the following few chapters we'll cover some of the other common employer-based retirement plans and the differences as compared to the 401(k). Some of these plans can be offered in conjunction with a 401(k) plan.

27. 403(b) Plans

The 403(b) plan is a defined contribution plan that is offered by not-for-profit organizations, religious organizations, and some governmental organizations. Often employees of hospitals, school districts, and nonprofit associations have a 403(b) plan as their choice to contribute to.

403(b) plans are very similar to 401(k) plans, since the 401(k) is much more common (even though the 403(b) has been around longer). Changes to 401(k) features over time are often used as a model for the rules of 403(b) plans. However, there are some differences that you need to understand if you have a 403(b) plan at your employer.

Contribution limits to a 403(b), for example, are identical to those for a 401(k). In fact, the annual limit for contributions ($20,500 plus $6,500 catch-up for 2022) is a combined limit for both 401(k) and 403(b). If you have two jobs and one offers a 403(b) while the other offers a 401(k), you have a single limit of $20,500 plus $6,500 if you're over age 50, for 2022. You could split the contributions between the two plans, or you could contribute the max to only one plan (and none to the other), or anything in between.

Investing within the 403(b) is virtually the same as with a 401(k) as well. Originally 403(b) plans were limited to only annuity-type investments, but that restriction has been removed and 403(b) plans can offer a wider variety of investment options, similar to a 401(k). 403(b) plans are restricted to investments that are qualified as a registered investment company under the 1940 Securities and Exchange Act. This limits the investment arena to publicly-traded mutual funds, annuities, and unit investment trusts (UITs). Individual stocks and bonds are not allowed in 403(b) plans.

A plan administrator may also choose to offer a Roth 403(b) plan with the regular 403(b). The rules and features for a Roth 403(b) are identical to the rules for a Roth 401(k).

Contributions to a 403(b) plan

For the most part, your contributions to a 403(b) are the same as with a 401(k). You sign up and elect to defer a certain amount (either dollars or a percentage) of your earnings into the 403(b). This amount is removed from your paycheck prior to tax calculations, and at the end of the year you only claim the non-deferred earnings on your tax return.

Many 403(b) plans do not include a company-matching contribution feature. This is primarily due to two factors: the entity is a non-profit (so no profits to share), and to avoid nondiscrimination testing. If the employer opts to provide matching contributions, this places the plan under the purview of ERISA. With ERISA oversight the plan must then comply with nondiscrimination testing along with certain other ERISA restrictions.

As a result, most 403(b) plans have no vesting schedule, since there are no matching funds in the account. If there are matching funds (and therefore the plan is ERISA-qualified), the vesting provisions are the same as with a 401(k).

Some 403(b) plans have a feature for participants with 15 or more years of service that provides for additional catch-up contributions, which is different from the 401(k). This provision (often referred to as MAC, or maximum allowable contribution) allows those employees to add an additional $3,000 to their annual contributions if they're under age 50. If over age 50, the regular catch-up provision allows a $6,500 additional contribution annually (for 2022).

The MAC feature is offered by relatively few 403(b) plans.

Distributions from 403(b) plans

The distribution rules for a 403(b) are identical to those for a 401(k) plan with one exception for RMDs. If you have more than one 403(b) plan from previous employers and you are over age 72, you are allowed to aggregate all of your 403(b) plans and take the RMD from only one plan if you choose.

If you'll recall, 401(k) plans require RMD to be calculated and taken individually from each plan that you own each year.

As with the 401(k), distributions of pre-tax amounts from your 403(b) plan are subject to ordinary income tax. If you withdraw money from the account before age 59½ (55 if you've left the company at or after that age), you will potentially have a 10% penalty applied to your distributions.

28. 457(b) (governmental) Plans

Many governmental units provide another type of retirement plan, called a 457(b) plan. Often 457(b) plans are referred to as "deferred comp" (for deferred compensation) plans. Many times, a 457(b) plan is offered as a savings option while the employer offers a primary retirement plan in the form of a pension arrangement.

Note: we are discussing specifically the 457(b) plan here. There is another type of 457 plan, called a 457(f) plan, which is only for highly-compensated employees of non-profits. It is possible to participate in both a 457(b) and a 457(f) plan at the same time. The 457(f) plan is less common, so we won't be covering it here.

The 457(b) plan has many similarities to the 401(k) plan – mechanics of participation are the same, investment choices are typically similar, and so on. There are several differences though, and you'll want to know about these because a 457(b) can be a real bonus if you are looking to add more money to your retirement savings.

A Roth 457(b) plan may also be offered by your employer (it's not required) which will have the same rules and features as a Roth 401(k) plan, except as noted below. The contribution and distribution differences apply to the Roth-type account as well.

Contributions to a 457(b) plan

Annual limits for contributions to a 457(b) plan are identical to those for 401(k) plans. However, your contributions to a 457(b) plan are not aggregated with 401(k) and 403(b) contributions to check against the annual limits. That is, if your employer offers both a 457(b) plan and either a 401(k) or 403(b) plan (not uncommon), you could contribute the maximum to both plans in a year.

This means that, for example, in 2022 you could contribute up to $20,500 to a 457(b) plan and another $20,500 to a 401(k) plan if you have both available. This brings your possible contribution to $41,000 for 2022. It doesn't matter if both plans are offered from the same employer or two different employers. (If you're over age 50 you can add the catch-up contribution to each plan, for an additional $13,000 on top of your $41,000 maximum contribution.)

In addition to the non-aggregation feature, some 457(b) plans have a way to super charge your contributions during the 3 years before normal retirement age (as defined by your plan administrator, often defaulted as age 65). If you have not maxed out your contributions in previous years, you may have the option of a special extra contribution of up to $20,500 (2022 figure) during your final 3 years of employment. This is on top of your regular contribution.

The special extra contribution is limited if you have made maximum contributions in prior years. It is eliminated altogether if you have utilized the age 50+ catch-up contribution in previous years.

Matching funds are usually not a feature of 457(b) plans, and so nondiscrimination testing is not required. In the rare instance that an employer provides contributions to the plan, unlike a 401(k) those contributions are counted toward your annual contribution limits. Vesting is also not typically a factor in a 457(b) plan either.

Distributions from a 457(b) plan

In addition to the differences with contributions, the really significant difference between a 457(b) and a 401(k) is in the distribution limitations. You are generally allowed to take distributions from a 457(b) plan without penalty at <u>any age</u> once you've left employment. This is huge, for some folks.

What this means is that you might work for a governmental entity for 20 years and then decide to move on to a private sector employer. No matter what age you are when you leave employment with the governmental entity, you can immediately withdraw funds from the 457(b) plan. You will have to pay ordinary income tax on the distribution of pre-tax money, but there will be no early distribution 10% penalty.

With that bonus feature, there is a downside: there are no in-service distributions allowed from a 457(b) plan until age 72. So, if you're still employed at the governmental entity, other than a hardship distribution, you don't have any option to take a withdrawal prior to age 72. But as mentioned above, no matter what age you are when you leave employment, you have unlimited access to the 457(b) account with no penalties.

Required Minimum Distributions (RMDs) begin for 457(b) plans when the participant reaches 72 years of age, just like a 401(k) plan.

29. Solo 401(k)

A Solo 401(k) is a special type of 401(k) plan that has only one participant, the owner of the business. The business must have no employees, other than your spouse (and your spouse can also participate in the Solo 401(k) as well, as long as he or she has compensation from the business).

Everything else about the account is just like a regular 401(k) from an employer. This is just a simplified plan for a sole proprietor. You can choose a Roth 401(k) and/or a traditional 401(k) plan for your contributions. Employer contributions must always be made to a traditional (non-Roth) 401(k) plan, however.

Contributions to the Solo 401(k) have the same limits as any other 401(k), but you have to consider that you're both the employee and the employer for the purpose of this plan.

So, as an employee, you have the $20,500 salary deferral contribution limit (plus the $6,500 catch up contribution if you're over age 50) in 2022. This deferral is limited to 100% of your compensation, so if you make less than $20,500, that's your limit.

As the employer however, you can make a profit-sharing contribution to the Solo 401(k) plan of up to 25% of your compensation or net self-employment income. Net self-employment income is your net profit minus ½ of your self-employment tax and your employee salary deferrals.

The total of all of your contributions to the Solo 401(k) plan is capped at $61,000 for 2022, plus $6,500 if you're over age 50.

These limitations are for ALL 401(k) plans that you participate in. If your self-employment is a side-gig and you're otherwise employed by an employer with a 401(k) plan, the total of all of your salary deferrals to all 401(k) plans cannot exceed the annual $20,500 limit (or $27,000 if over age 50).

If you have the opportunity to start your own business – such as consulting, or perhaps another part-time business – you can start your own Solo 401(k) plan and rollover the funds from your old plan(s) and IRAs if you have them. Then, on the chance that you'd need the money later on after you're at least age 55 (but not yet 59½), assuming that you can end your employment in your consultancy or other self-employment activity, you can then have access to those funds in your Solo 401(k) plan without penalty.

If you go the self-employment route, you need to make sure that the business that you've created is valid and legitimate. The IRS doesn't at all take this lightly – if your business isn't making money (or at least validly attempting to make money), your actions in creating a 401(k) plan and everything else associated with the business can be considered fraud.

This also applies to the dissolution of the business in order to have access to the retirement funds. If it's deemed that the only reason you did this was simply to have access, this action could be considered fraud as well. This could come about if you dissolved the original business and then shortly afterward started a similar business again, for example.

30. Inherited 401(k) Plan

An inherited 401(k) plan isn't necessarily a different kind of retirement plan from a regular 401(k) plan in the hands of the original participant. However, the rules around an inherited 401(k) plan are unusual enough to warrant their own review.

When an individual inherits a 401(k) plan, generally this individual must take distributions from the plan, on a preset schedule. There are a few things to consider, the first of which is whether the beneficiary is the spouse of the original owner, or another person (non-spouse).

If the beneficiary is a spouse, special options are available for handling the inherited 401(k) plan. As a spouse-beneficiary, you have 3 primary options to choose from:

1. You can leave the money in the 401(k) plan.

2. You can rollover the money from the 401(k) plan to an inherited IRA.

3. You can rollover the money from the 401(k) plan into an IRA in your own name or another 401(k) (this is different from option #2).

If you inherit a 401(k) plan from someone other than your spouse, you are limited to either #1 or #2 above. We'll go over the three options in detail next.

Leave the money in the 401(k) plan

If you choose to leave your inherited 401(k) in the original account, you now have to withdraw the entire amount within 10 years, unless you're a spouse of the original owner or one of the excepted beneficiaries, which includes a minor child of the original owner, a chronically ill or disabled dependent of the original owner, or a beneficiary who is not more than 10 years younger than the original owner.

When withdrawing the account over 10 years, you don't have to take a specific amount out annually, you just need to distribute the entire account within 10 years, beginning with the year following the year of the death of the original owner.

The rule is different if you are the spouse of the original owner.

If you are the spouse of the original owner, you have the option of delaying until the original owner would have been 72 years old before taking the RMDs. In this case, the RMDs would be based on the decedent's assumed age (had he or she still been living) in each year of distribution.

If you are a non-spouse beneficiary, the default rule is that you must withdraw the entire amount of the 401(k) account by December 31 of the tenth year following the year that the original owner died. You can take some money out each year, or take it all at once, it just has to be withdrawn before the end of the tenth year.

If you are one of the other excepted beneficiaries (besides the spouse), you can use your lifetime as the payout period for taking distributions from the inherited plan. This means that you must take a specific amount (or more) out of the account each year, beginning with the year following the death of the original owner.

In all cases, you have the option of taking more than the minimum out of the account each year. In none of these cases will you have a 10% penalty applied for early distribution, but you will owe income tax on all pre-tax money withdrawn.

Rollover the inherited 401(k) to an inherited IRA

If you choose instead to rollover the inherited 401(k) to an inherited IRA, you have a bit more flexibility, but only a bit. Not all plans allow this rollover option – some plans are more restrictive and force non-spouse beneficiaries to only use the 10-year complete payout option detailed previously.

As before when leaving the money in the 401(k) account, you must withdraw the entire balance from the inherited IRA (which you rolled over the 401(k) plan to) within 10 years of the death of the original owner.

Certain classes of individuals may be eligible to stretch the distribution period, whether from the original 401(k) or an inherited IRA. These include the spouse of the original owner, a child of the original owner who is under the (state-specific) age of majority, a dependent beneficiary who is disabled or chronically ill, or a beneficiary who is not more than 10 years younger than the original owner.

In the case of the child beneficiary, he or she may take RMDs based upon Table I (see IRS Publication 590) until reaching the age of majority. Upon reaching majority, this beneficiary must distribute the account over the coming 10-year period.

In all cases concerning the excepted beneficiaries, upon the death of this beneficiary, the 10-year payout rule applies to whomever the successor beneficiary may be.

Rollover the inherited 401(k) to your own IRA

This option is <u>only</u> available for a spouse beneficiary.

As a spouse, you have the option of rolling over the 401(k) plan to an IRA in your own name (not an inherited IRA). This action can cause restrictions that you may not want, but it could open up flexibility as well.

If you are under age $59\frac{1}{2}$ and are the spouse beneficiary, rolling over the inherited 401(k) plan to your own IRA will eliminate your ability to withdraw funds from the account without penalty, unless you meet one of the exceptions for early withdrawal from an IRA. Once you reach age $59\frac{1}{2}$ or an exception applies, you will be able to access the money without penalties. It's important to note that this rollover action does completely eliminate your ability to withdraw funds without penalty before age $59\frac{1}{2}$. As mentioned previously, if you leave the money in the inherited 401(k) account you would have access to the money without penalty no matter what your age.

If you're between 59½ and 72 years old, rolling over the inherited 401(k) to your own IRA can give you more flexibility. By doing this rollover, if your late spouse was already subject to RMDs, you can delay RMDs now until you reach age 72. This is because the account is no longer associated with your late spouse – it's your IRA. You also can freely withdraw any amount for any purpose and only pay ordinary income tax on the distribution, no early withdrawal penalty will apply.

If you're over age 72 and you rollover the inherited 401(k) plan to your own IRA, you must take RMDs based on your lifetime and the account balance in your IRA.

As before, except for the case where you're under age 59½ (when penalty-free withdrawals are not allowed), you are allowed to take more than the minimum distribution each year, but you must at least take the minimum.

Roth Conversion of Inherited 401(k)

One of the provisions that is available to the individual who inherits a 401(k) or other Qualified Retirement Plan (QRP) is the ability to convert the fund to a Roth IRA.

This gives the beneficiary of the original QRP the option of having all of the tax paid up front on the account, and then all growth in the account in the future is tax free, as with all Roth IRA accounts.

What's a bit different about this kind of conversion is that, since it came from an inherited account, the non-excepted beneficiary must still withdraw the entire amount from the account within 10 years.

A downside to this move is that the heir should also be in a position to pay the tax on the conversion from other funds, otherwise the tax pulled from the account (and therefore not converted to Roth) will reduce the funds that can grow tax-free over time.

If the heir has an IRA of his or her own that could be converted, and there are only enough other funds for paying tax to enable the conversion of one account or the other, the IRA should be converted rather than the 401(k). This is because the IRA has a much better chance for long-term growth than the inherited QRP due to the requirement for distribution of the account (as discussed above).

This is yet another reason that an individual might want to leave funds in a 401(k) plan rather than rolling it over to an IRA – since the heir does not have this Roth conversion option available if the money is in an inherited IRA. This option is only available for an inherited 401(k).

Inherited Roth 401(k)

If the account that you've inherited is a Roth 401(k), if you leave it in the original Roth 401(k) account, you'll need to take distribution of the entire balance within

10 years. (The excepted beneficiaries can still stretch the payouts over their lifetimes as with the inherited traditional 401(k) plan.)

You could also rollover the Roth 401(k) to an inherited Roth IRA (similar to the conversion described previously). This is a tax-free event since the money is coming from an account that has already been treated as Roth with contributions. Distribution within 10 years is still required as if the money was still in the Roth 401(k) account.

As a spouse, you further have the option of rollover of the account to a Roth IRA in your own name (not an inherited Roth IRA). This would eliminate the RMD requirement during your lifetime.

Excepted beneficiaries (child, chronically ill or disabled, or not more than 10 years younger) may stretch out the payments from the plan over their lifetimes. In the case of the child, the stretch using lifetime amortization only applies until the child reaches the age of majority – after which the 10-year payout rule applies.

31. Other Retirement Plans

There are several other types of retirement plans that have similarities to 401(k) plans, and we've listed a few of these below. This is not an exhaustive list by any means, but should represent the most common plans that you may come across.

Thrift Savings Plan (TSP)

The Thrift Savings Plan, or TSP, is the US federal government's equivalent of a 401(k) plan. Many features of the TSP are identical to the 401(k) plan.

For example, TSP has a tax-deductible and a Roth option; the contribution limits are identical to 401(k) plans; upon leaving employment, TSP accounts can be rolled over to an IRA or another employer-based plan; and TSP allows for in-service distributions and loans, just like 401(k) plans. TSP also allows rollovers from outside retirement plans (like an IRA or a previous employer's 401(k) plan).

Investment options in TSP are very limited. However, the available options provide good diversification across asset classes and are very low cost investments. Most of the investment choices are indexes, which provide great diversification with low costs. These indexes are not publicly-traded but are similar to other publicly-traded indexes.

The federal government provides an automatic 1% contribution to TSP for all employees, and they will match up to an additional 4% if the employee contributes 5% of salary.

Upon retirement, the participant is allowed partial or full distribution from the plan. When the participant reaches age 72, RMDs are required, just the same as with a 401(k). This age may be deferred if the participant is still employed as of age 72. If this is the case, RMDs begin the year after leaving employment.

For more information on TSP, go to www.TSP.gov.

Keogh

Ah, the poor, misunderstood and neglected Keogh (KEE-og) Plan. You don't get the press that your fancy relatives 401(k), IRA and Roth, or even SIMPLE achieve... it seems as if the investment discussion world is completely abandoning you.

First brought into existence in 1962 (yes, it's a late-boomer like me!) the Keogh or HR10 plan is essentially a vehicle that allows the self-employed to establish pension plans just like the big companies can. A Keogh plan can be either a defined benefit (traditional pension) or a defined contribution (like a 401(k)) plan.

The Keogh plan has many of the same attributes as 401(k) plans, including the age 59½ limit for qualified withdrawals, as well as the age 72 required minimum distribution rules. Depending upon the type of plan established, you can invest in most common investment vehicles within a Keogh plan.

Other Retirement Plans

The real benefit of a Keogh plan over a SIMPLE or other type of plan available to small employers is in the higher limit for contributions. In the Keogh plan, up to $61,000 (for 2022) can be contributed and deducted, limited to 25% of the overall compensation of the employee.

Alternative retirement plan vehicles such as the solo 401(k) plan have lessened the need for the Keogh plans in the defined contribution arena. However, for establishment of a defined benefit pension plan or a money purchase pension plan, the Keogh remains a very important piece of the puzzle for sole proprietorships and other unincorporated businesses.

One particular downside to the Keogh plan: If you have no employees, your Keogh plan is not necessarily protected from creditors. If there are employees in the plan (other than owner/partners) then ERISA law protects the accounts from creditors. But without employees, ERISA has no jurisdiction over these accounts, and your assets may be subject to creditor claims, depending upon applicable state laws. Just something to keep in mind with the Keogh.

You're eligible to participate in a Keogh retirement plan if you are:

- self-employed, a small business owner, or an active partner in an unincorporated business who performs personal services for the company, or

- a sole proprietor who files Schedule C, or

- in a partnership whose members file Schedule E (in this case, the partnership, not you, must establish the Keogh plan), or

- working for another company, but working for your own business as well (for example, if you're a writer with another day job and you're earning royalties on your first book, the royalties count as self-employment income)

You are not eligible to participate in a Keogh plan if you are:

- a salaried worker for an incorporated business, with no other source of income, or

- retired and not receiving compensation from a business, or

- an unpaid volunteer at the business that offers the plan

SEP IRA

Simplified Employee Pension (SEP) IRAs are retirement plans designed for small businesses to provide a retirement plan for employees (if there are employees). The SEP IRA is a type of IRA, so it's not subject to the ERISA rules that 401(k) plans are, but the IRS has adopted very similar rules to apply to the SEP IRA plans.

With a SEP, only the employer makes contributions to the plan, the employee doesn't defer income into the plan. The employer contributions are always 100% vested to the employee, however.

As a self-employed individual, you have similar options with a SEP IRA as you do with a Solo 401(k) plan: up to the lesser of 25% of net earnings, or $61,000 (for 2022). There is no catch-up provision for the SEP IRA.

There is no option for loans from a SEP IRA, nor is there a Roth option. SEP IRAs do not allow for in-plan distributions – you must leave the employer in order to access the funds in the account.

Otherwise, distributions from a SEP IRA are similar to a regular IRA, in that all amounts within the account will have ordinary income tax applied upon distribution. If you take an early distribution and you don't meet one of the exceptions, a 10% penalty will apply to your distribution as well.

SIMPLE IRA/401(k)

SIMPLE plans (stands for Savings Incentive Match PLan for Employees, yes, this is an elusive backronym in the wild!) are retirement plans specifically for small businesses with fewer than 100 employees. To count as one of the 100 employees, the employee has received at least $5,000 in compensation over the previous year.

SIMPLE IRA and SIMPLE 401(k) are very similar, each providing for employee deferral of salary, along with matching contributions from the employer. The limit for employee deferrals for 2022 is $14,000, with a

$3,000 catch up contribution allowed if the employee is age 50 or better.

An employee must be at least 21 years of age before participation in a SIMPLE 401(k). The SIMPLE IRA has no age limit.

Company matching contributions to SIMPLE 401(k) and SIMPLE IRA plans are done either by a prescribed match, dollar-for-dollar up to 3%, or a non-elective 2% contribution for all employees, regardless of whether the employee is deferring wages into the plan. Employees are immediately 100% vested in all company matching contributions of either type.

For the SIMPLE IRA only, if the employer has chosen to make matching contributions, the match can be reduced from the prescribed 3% to as little as 1% (but no less) for two out of every five years. This option is not available for the SIMPLE 401(k).

Nondiscrimination rules do not apply to either the SIMPLE IRA or the SIMPLE 401(k), since the matching is done on a prescribed basis.

Money in a SIMPLE plan is restricted from rollover into other types of plans for the first two years of the plan's existence (for each employee). After that, rollovers are allowed.

Plan loans may be available to participants in a SIMPLE 401(k), much the same as a traditional 401(k) plan. On the other hand, SIMPLE IRA participants do not have access (in any way) to the funds in the

SIMPLE IRA prior to leaving employment or reaching age 59½.

Both the SIMPLE 401(k) and SIMPLE IRA can allow a designated Roth account option.

Part 7: Conclusion

32. Did the Advent of 401(k) Plans Hurt Americans?

A few years ago, the Economic Policy Institute produced a study, "Rise of 401(k)s Hurt More Americans Than It Helped". As the title implies, the study indicates that the 401(k) plan itself is the cause of America's lack of retirement resources. Personally, I think it has more to do with the fact that the 401(k) plans (and other defined contribution plans) were expected to be a *replacement* for the old-style defined benefit pension plans, and the fact that those administering the retirement plans did little to ensure success for the employees.

Traditional defined benefit pension plans didn't ask the employee to decide how much to set aside – this was determined by actuaries. Then the company made sure that the money was set aside (in most cases) so that the promised benefit would be there when the employee retires. In the world of 401(k) plans, the employee has free choice to decide how much to fund, and in fact whether or not to fund the retirement plan at all. Human nature kicks in, and the nearer term needs of the employee win out over long term needs – of course the long-term requirements (e.g., retirement savings) often get short shrift!

It's the same as when we turn over the car keys to a 16-year-old. Up to this point, the child has just ridden along, not having to know anything about rules of the road, car maintenance, or paying attention to directions or other vehicles around him. You wouldn't just toss Johnny the keys and say "You know where you want to go. Do your best to get there!" Of course, you're going to make sure that he has all the training necessary to operate the vehicle safely, and that he knows when to put fuel in the car, as well as that he knows how to navigate to his destination on time.

If the playing field had been level – that is, if when 401(k)-type plans were introduced as true replacements for pension plans – that there was no choice regarding participation and funding level, we'd see a much different picture. I don't think education alone is the answer, because the importance of continual funding is so difficult to comprehend, and so critical to success. Forced participation runs counter to the "American Way", but that would have changed our outlook dramatically.

The problem isn't the 401(k) plan itself. The problem is that when companies dropped pension plans in favor of 401(k) plans, they didn't provide employees with the correct message about the importance of participation. Free will is a good thing, don't get me wrong. But I think employers could have done much, much more to emphasize the importance of participation, of making long-term investment decisions, and of providing for the future with today's earnings. It's not the 401(k) itself that is the problem, it's in the implementation.

33. Future of the 401(k) plan

As of 2019, the most significant legislation pertaining to the future of retirement plans in several years has been passed by Congress. The SECURE Act (Setting Every Community Up for Retirement Enhancement) made the first major changes to the retirement plan landscape since the Economic Growth and Tax Relief Reconciliation Act of 2001 (EGTRRA).

Five of the most significant changes that the SECURE Act has are:

1. Increasing the Required Minimum Distribution Age to 72 (from 70½).

2. Removing the age at which you must stop making contributions to your IRA. Just the same as with 401(k) plans, if you're working and earning income, you can contribute to an IRA at any age with this legislation.

3. Strict limitation of the stretch provision to no more than 10 years after the original account owner's death (with a few excepted beneficiaries, including spouses).

4. Small employers may now band together in order to achieve economies of scale to offer 401(k) plans to their employees.

5. Easing of restrictions to allow employers to offer annuities as an option for investment of 401(k) plan contributions.

The first two items are relatively trivial. Sure, it's an extended time for allowable contributions, and you can delay distributions for 18 months. In the grand scheme of things, I doubt seriously if these two changes will have any significant impact.

The third item, which effectively eliminates the stretch provision as a long-term planning tool for non-excepted beneficiaries, is likely to have a significant impact. Under current rules, a retirement plan (IRA or 401(k) plan) could have a very significant lifespan, potentially providing a legacy for many years and generations after the death of the original owner.

Spouse (and the other excepted) beneficiaries of retirement plans are not impacted by this provision unless they choose to maintain the account as "inherited". If they take on the account as their own plan or maintain the account with no changes, they are still allowed to distribute the plan over the lifetime of the original owner or the surviving spouse's lifetime, without the 10-year limitation.

It is anticipated that this change will produce up to $16 billion in additional tax revenues over the coming decade, so you can see that the impact to taxpayers will be significant.

The ability of small employers to band together to offer 401(k) plans may be beneficial in the long run, although I wonder just how many small employers will be compelled to seek out these options. Time will tell.

Conclusion

The last item in my list, that of allowing employers to offer annuities as an option for participant investments, may be a good thing, or it may be the worst of all.

The concept seems to favor participants – giving them the option of utilizing an annuity within the 401(k) plan to potentially produce long-term retirement income, similar to old-style pension plans. For example, instead of saving money toward an ill-defined lump sum target in retirement, with the annuity option the participant could readily plan toward a specific income target.

There's a reason that the average individual typically doesn't seek out annuities as a retirement savings alternative. Annuities are, on the whole, some of the most expensive, complex and illiquid financial products ever created. The average individual 401(k) plan participant has little chance of fully understanding all of the costs, implications, and issues with annuities. Too often, an annuity is chosen because a salesman has presented it, not because the investor has taken the time to fully understand it in the context of alternatives.

The problem with this provision is that the employee has no protection against predatory annuity sales. You see, annuities have always been an option to offer within a 401(k) plan, but under current law if the annuity provider were to go out of business or defraud the participants, the participants would be allowed to sue the plan provider (employer) for any losses. This new provision in the SECURE Act removes that responsibility from the employer – effectively taking away a protection from the employee/participant.

The SECURE Act seems to have been set up with the primary aim of opening up the 401(k) plan landscape to insurance companies with no restrictions. There is even a provision in the Act that requires plan administrators to annually produce a "lifetime income disclosure" to participants. Effectively this is a plan-endorsed advertisement for the annuity company, and even though it's described as an annual report, I would be shocked if this wasn't built-in as a regular feature, providing real-time projections.

Topping it off, there is no recourse for the employee if the projections provided were overly optimistic. Employers are legally protected against any lawsuits arising from such issues as a part of the SECURE Act.

Without more complete education (which is of course not required), it's not hard to imagine that annuity sales will increase under this scenario. When the employee/participant in a 401(k) plan is constantly reminded of the monthly income that their plan account could provide if they transfer everything to an annuity, of course that's going to seem like a logical step. It may even seem as if that's the step that is expected of you, endorsed by the plan administrator, although you have many other options to consider.

It is very early in the timeline to understand all of the provisions of the SECURE Act, and we'll incorporate more planning options in future editions as they become apparent.

34. Integrating the 401(k) Into Your Financial Plan

Now that you've begun deferring money into your 401(k) plan, it's time to fit this saving activity into your retirement planning process.

At a high level, this is accomplished by reviewing your monthly expenditures (the expected expenses in your future retirement) and comparing that amount with the sources of income that you can expect in retirement.

The process is mostly a math exercise, but there are matters that you'll need to account for that you might not be thinking of. These include the effect of inflation on both your sources of income and your expenses, as well as tax implications on the sources of income.

Various income sources have widely-varying tax implications. For example, Social Security benefits may be included as taxable at as high as an 85% rate, but they may be included at a lower rate or completely tax-free. Included in the tax-free list would be your Roth IRA and Roth 401(k) disbursements. Withdrawals of regular IRA or 401(k) funds are generally taxed at your ordinary income tax rate (and depending on your age, might be subject to a penalty as well). Non-deferred accounts, such as bank accounts or brokerage accounts, are only taxed to the extent of the growth of the account, and may be taxed at (currently) favorable capital gains rates.

Inflation's impact to your income sources is another area that needs much review. Failing to expose your savings to investments that will keep up with or exceed the rate of inflation will eventually erode the buying power.

For example, if you placed all of your money in a standard bank savings account paying 0.5% interest and inflation is 2% per year, each year that passes erodes the buying power of your savings by 1.5%, and this erosion compounds over time.

Inflation will also gradually increase the cost of your living expenses. The overall inflation rate lately has been in the 2-3% range annually, however inflation on certain items has been significantly higher at times. Healthcare expenses are a good example of this higher rate of inflation, with a long-term average above 5%.

Healthcare insurance is a matter that many early retirees fail to completely understand the impact. This is especially true if your retirement occurs before you reach age 65, the age of Medicare eligibility. Depending upon your income, pre-Medicare health insurance purchased privately (not through an employer or group plan) can be very costly.

All of these factors must be reviewed in the context of your needs and sources in order to plan a retirement that will be free of concern over running out of money. Consult a fee-only financial advisor to help you work through the details of such a financial plan. You'll be glad you did.

www.ingramcontent.com/pod-product-compliance
Lightning Source LLC
Chambersburg PA
CBHW070628220526
45466CB00001B/122